CONNECT WITH YOUR HORSE FROM THE GROUND UP

Transform the Way You See, "Feel," and Ride with a Whole New Kind of Groundwork

Peggy Cummings with Bobbie Jo Lieberman

Foreword by Linda Tellington-Jones

TRAFALGAR SQUARE
North Pomfret, Vermont

First published in 2011 by
Trafalgar Square Books
North Pomfret, Vermont 05053

Printed in China

Library of Congress Cataloging-in-Publication Data

Cummings, Peggy.
Connect with your horse from the ground up : transform the way you see, feel, and ride with a whole new kind of groundwork / Peggy Cummings with Bobbie Jo Lieberman.
p. cm.
Includes index.
ISBN 978-1-57076-422-6
1. Horses--Training. 2. Horses--Behavior. I. Lieberman, Bobbie. II. Title.
SF287.C84 2011
636.1'0835--dc22
2010042786

All photos courtesy of Peggy Cummings
Illustrations by Nancy Camp and cartoons by Sally Spencer

Book design by Carrie Fradkin
Cover design by RM Didier
Typefaces: ITC Century, Helvetica

10 9 8 7 6 5 4 3 2 1

DEDICATION

I dedicate this book to my equine mentors: King (my first love); Tiffany; Crystal; Scotia (my beloved "professor"); Valdai; Party; and Belle. These horses made it clear to me that they could not perform under saddle to their potential without being reschooled from the ground first. They gave me the gift of the "why" of Connected Groundwork®.

I also dedicate this book to my riding master, Skipper Bartlett, who taught me to "ride" horses from the ground; to Laurel Marshfield, who let me teach her to ride King while I worked him from the ground; and to Linda Tellington-Jones and her sister Robyn Hood. Linda and Robyn have supported my journey to keep seeking ways to help horses "come through" in motion from the ground before being ridden. Robyn has adapted Connected Groundwork for working with companion animals and combined it with the Tellington Method for amazing results with horses. I deeply respect their contribution to bridging human and animal understanding, communication, and cooperation.

CONTENTS

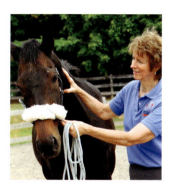

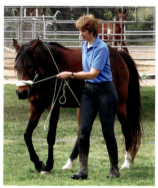

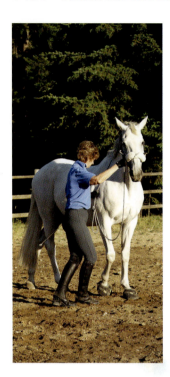

A century ago, learning how to work with horses was still a necessary part of daily life. Fifty years ago, after the necessity for "work horses" subsided, riding—for sport and recreation—began to rise again. Performance and competition tend to take the spotlight; however, the horse's ultimate role on our planet may yet be unfolding.

Nearly every day I encounter people who have become estranged from the world of nature. They see involvement with horses as an opportunity to once again be immersed in the flow of life and come back into contact with themselves as part of the natural world. More and more people are turning to riding as a recreational activity that reconnects them with nature. In today's world there are millions of pleasure riders—the number one equestrian activity—as involvement with our equine friends becomes ever more important for our physical and emotional well-being.

Young people and adults alike learn from horses to love creation, and to celebrate and appreciate nature and all living creatures. They practice patience and devotion to a task, learn to sense their own power, and also to face their fears. They experience speed, movement, beauty, and the ability to learn. Through the horse they experience the world with all their senses. These are but a few examples of the many great gifts life has to offer human beings. So many participants in my courses, thoroughly moved by their experience, have thanked a horse for helping them to see with new eyes the most essential qualities of life.

Today the demands—and expectations—of working with horses are different than they were a hundred years ago. The art of horsemanship is no longer simply about learning specific movements. Of course we want to learn how we can influence a horse harmoniously and without force, but our experience with horses should also help us to attain the best possible expression of ourselves. The goal is a pleasurable leisure time activity that enhances our further development as grounded human beings.

With this book, in addition to Connected Riding, the reader has a gem before her—one that prepares the way for a special relationship between human and horse. But this book also helps you make great strides in interpreting the principles of classical riding and incorporating them correctly into the ridden work you do with your horse.

About 25 years ago, I got to know Peggy as one of my most enthusiastic students. She was a young, talented woman nearly obsessed with the desire to understand the horse. Whenever she had a new way to help a horse improve his body posture or his movement, there was no holding her back. Her knowledge and creativity nearly bubble over now, as they did then. At the same time, I know Peggy as a passionate teacher. If, at the end of a long work day, when she is exhaustedly packing her things away, one presents Peggy with another rider and horse, she immerses herself in their problems and questions for another couple of hours to show the rider how she can best support the horse and best use her own body to work in connection with the horse.

I also know Peggy as a woman who walks her own path. Even as the mother of six splendid children, there was no keeping her from fulfilling her mission toward horses and people.

Peggy's work is a treasure I urge readers to take to heart. It is a weaving together of classical riding teachings, paths to self-discovery, methods of learning, body-awareness exercises, knowledge of biomechanics, and creative ways of teaching the complexities of the art of riding. Sophisticated yet simple concepts for the development of the body open the way to an emotional balance in both human and horse—as students of the Tellington Method® have long known and also experienced.

When we work with horses it becomes very clear that everything can change from one moment to the next. The bodies of rider and horse are never static—the trick is to find moments of balance over and over again. This premise seems so logical, yet we nevertheless usually proceed from the assumption that rider and horse must remain in constant balance. Peggy's techniques support the horse in seeking his balance during groundwork, and then both rider and horse finding such balance and connection more and more often.

Connected Groundwork, like Connected Riding, is based on the concept of connection. Peggy presents a method that connects the horse from back to front and connects the rider from toe to head. It also embodies connection of body, mind, and spirit, as well as connection between horse and rider, all given to us by a talented and extraordinary teacher. The two sister methods, my Tellington Method and Peggy's work, share stunningly similar basic principles: awareness of and respect for the horse as a living being; self-carriage, self-control, and self-awareness as a goal; building a deep relationship; and respect for the learner and his/her individuality, whether horse or human. Peggy never forgets to recommend the Tellington Method to her students as foundation work. Turning the tables, I would like to recommend that all enthusiasts of my work explore Connected Groundwork and Riding. Whether you are new to horses, a seasoned veteran, or an instructor, Peggy's work will take you to the next level. I wish you much success in "feeling within"—into yourself and into your friend, the horse—so that you will come to have a deeper connection with one another.

Linda Tellington-Jones
Kailua-Kona, Hawaii

In this book I share some of the insights I have gleaned over the past 35 years—specific principles that have made a difference in the way I look at horses move and how I help them become better riding horses by working them from the ground. I offer you an understanding of why horses become unbalanced, get "stuck," and have evasions, and provide techniques to "unstick" and free up their movement by working them from the ground for better performance.

Effortless flying lead changes, smoother transitions, better lateral work and an all-around happier horse—one that is able to truly move forward—are just some of the results my students and I have seen time after time.

Tightness, bracing patterns, crookedness, and on-the-forehand tendencies exist in all horses. Some have these patterns from birth. Others begin acquiring them as soon as a halter is put on their head, a bit goes into their mouth, and a rider gets on their back. The groundwork exercises in this book—which form the prelude and foundation to my Connected Riding method—have restored movement, function, and elasticity to hundreds of horses worldwide.

The exercises in this book will help *you*:

→ Understand your horse's behavior and movement patterns.

→ Use your body more efficiently to facilitate response and change in your horse.

→ See and feel how you can help your horse develop his "lifting" and "pushing" muscles.

→ Assess what your horse needs *today*.

Connected Groundwork helps *your horse*:

→ Let go of tension, tightness, and bracing patterns.

→ Develop focus, willingness, and participation.

→ Engage his working muscles before being ridden.

→ Maintain core muscle strength when ridden and at liberty.

→ Keep his back lifted and his hind end engaged.

→ Develop his "pushing power."

→ Overcome bracing patterns that inhibit performance and learning.

→ Use both sides of his body with equal freedom and balance.

→ Overcome common "resistances" such as bucking, bolting, balking, and rearing.

→ Shift his weight in movement dynamically in three dimensions: back to front, down to up, side to side.

→ Reciprocate by maintaining connection and taking responsibility for carrying himself.

→ Achieve his full potential in freedom of movement.

Connected Groundwork exercises not only loosen, reeducate, and strengthen your horse's body, they give you keen assessment tools that tell you a great deal about the state of your horse's mind and body—and how he is likely to respond under saddle or on the Connected Groundwork "line" each day. Whether you take a few weeks or months to work through the exercises in this book or do a few each day before you ride, you will see a difference immediately in your horse's response, acceptance, and willingness.

I offer this book to you and your horse with confidence that the exercises will change the way you see and feel your horse and improve how he moves in his body. I deeply wish for it to bring you and your horse many years of connection and joy together. Connected Groundwork prepares you and your horse for whatever you want to do each day and paves the way for a more harmonious riding experience. It is both a journey and an end in itself; a diagnostic tool; a schooling aid; and a preventive health measure. Above all, it is a way to *connect* with your horse—and he to you—at a level that goes far beyond obedience and conditioned response. It is based on biomechanical and physiological laws, but at its heart, it is acknowledging the soul-deep connection that can be possible when two beings come together without fear or tension.

It is my hope that this book is the beginning of your journey toward true connection with your horse!

Peggy Cummings

The first important horse in my life was a 15.2-hand, bay gelding out of Canada named King, who had been intended for the New York City police force. I had the good fortune to attend a private high school in a small town in Maine where riding and horsemanship were part of the core curriculum. As a high school freshman I fell in love with King but was not allowed to ride him because he was considered the most difficult horse in the barn.

I wanted so badly to ride this challenging, misunderstood horse that people called "bad" when he only was struggling to express himself. I worked hard to earn the privilege of riding King, and in my sophomore year my riding master, Clarence D. "Skipper" Bartlett, saw my determination and absolute dedication, and finally decided to let me do so.

I spent endless hours with King—grooming him, touching him all over his body, and enjoying games of hide-and-seek (I'd rattle candy wrappers so he would come find me). We played together, and he would come when I called. Eventually, King "allowed me" to ride him—I'd ride him bareback, sometimes standing up on his back and wiggling my legs, and he would trot around the arena. We became friends, and he learned to trust me. In my eyes, he was beautiful, and I loved his spirit.

King would do just about anything for me, including flying lead changes. He had full, round, easy-moving gaits. Although King initially had some "kinks" in his body, he became more and more supple and became one of the top school horses in Skipper's string over the next two years.

King's Teachings: Finding the Happy, Free Horse Within

King taught me the value of spending a lot of time touching a horse all over his body. In those days, horses typically stood in tie-stalls with little or no turnout and only arena riding for exercise. He needed a break—mentally and physically—from feeling confined, and some time to rebuild his trust with people. I intuitively knew that once he was happier, we could work together in a different way.

Because King, like all the horses I rode in high school, had some stiffness and bracing patterns, he taught me that to ride him well, I had to ride his walk-trot transitions in a softer way than was the norm. He helped me recognize sensations of stiffness and inhibited movement in horses.

Although I had the opportunity to ride horses capable of high-level movements, I became disillusioned feeling how hard they were to ride and how much strength was required to get them to perform. The words I kept hearing from teachers included "lightness" and "ease," yet so many of these horses seemed mechanical and shut down—lifeless. I was horrified by the rigidity and bracing patterns in the school horses.

For King to be kept for the school, I had to make him safe and cooperative for others to ride in our program. A younger student—a "little sister" of mine—let me give her a riding lesson while I "rode" King from the ground. This is the work that "saved" King by helping him learn to become a reliable teacher. In retrospect, this was a pivotal moment in the beginning of my life's mission.

The Alexander Technique

The Alexander Technique is a method that works to change (movement) habits in our everyday activities. It is a simple and practical method for improving ease and freedom of movement, balance, support, and coordination. The technique teaches the use of the appropriate amount of effort for a particular activity, giving you more energy for all that you do. It is not a series of treatments or exercises but rather a reeducation of the mind and body. The Alexander Technique helps a person discover a new balance in the body by releasing unnecessary tension. It can be applied to sitting, lying down, standing, walking, lifting, and other daily activities.

—From *Changing the Way You Work: The Alexander Technique* (www.alexandertechnique.com)

The Link between Physical Well-Being and Attitude

Years later, when King was 18 and I was 26, he was given to me by Bartlett. By then King had lost much of his elasticity and was stiff; his stride no longer had spring—I felt as if I was riding a deflated basketball with no bounce. He had lost his forward movement and the fullness of his stride, and he was unwilling. What I learned over the next three years was how to get all he once was, back.

I knew we had to begin again, helping him to recover trust, playfulness, and movement in his body. I turned him out in a large paddock in our backyard, and for the first time he enjoyed the freedom of being able to move at liberty and socialize with other horses. Having been a school horse for 12 years, the years of service had taken their toll. He was cranky and antisocial. Dogs and small children beware! He spent the first winter being cared for by two young girls that doted on him and rode him in a small field. By the following summer his stride was freer, and he was much more pleasant to be around. Through the course of three years of turnout and being ridden outside an arena, King's entire way of going and

personality were transformed—from shutdown, crabby, and unwilling, to willing, playful, and curious.

King's biggest lesson to me was that it is possible to find the happy horse within by (re)creating movement in the body. By letting go of bracing patterns and stiffness, the mind and attitude can find a new sense of freedom, too.

By the early 1970s, I realized that if I spent time with horses on the ground—walking them in curved patterns, touching them, feeling their body for tightness—they became happier, more willing horses. Sally Swift. creator of Centered Riding®, used to say she loved coming to my barn because the horses in it weren't typical school horses. I became known in my community as the one who would take horses nobody wanted or couldn't figure out. Each one of them had lessons to teach me about undoing bracing patterns and resolving behavior issues.

Improving Horses' Comfort and Freedom of Motion

I was fortunate to have many accomplished competition horses in my barn over the years, and I was dismayed at how stiff and unsound some were when they arrived. I sought to find ways that would improve their comfort and freedom of motion so that the work they did would be *joyful* instead of *dutiful*. I sensed it had to be something other than bad training or handling that made horses sour, untrustworthy, and unenthusiastic in their work.

Transmitting Awareness and Lightness to the Horse's Body

Many of these horses had difficulty with specific movements—turn on the forehand, picking up a lead, and walk-trot transitions, for example. I would dismount, move the horse in different directions, touch his body seeking out discomfort or stiffness, and try to figure out where the limitation was. When I remounted invariably I found the horse was much looser and able to achieve what I was asking.

When I began traveling and teaching clinics, I found many horses so stiff in the arena that their riders could not feel details of their movement. At that time I was teaching people to ride with more awareness, lightness, and softness in their body, and it became really obvious to me that I needed to find some ways to provide the same relief for the horses.

Another of my "aha" moments came in 1978 when my mother gave me two Hungarian horses, one of which had serious bucking, bolting, and spooking issues. I sent the horse away twice to professional trainers, and both times he came back lame. This led me to question the traditional ways that horses were trained and schooled. It seemed the horse's body was being overlooked as a component of the riding equation.

In 1981 I purchased Scotia, a Percheron/Thoroughbred cross from Nova Scotia who was to be my competition horse. A serious trailer accident left him unable to be under saddle for a year due to hip injuries. I now believe Scotia came off that trailer and into my life to ensure I chose a new path with horses and people. In order to remain sound under saddle, Scotia required loosening in his body before I could ride him. My work with him led me to Sally Swift, Linda Tellington-Jones, Jack Meagher, and other alternative practitioners—for both of us. I finally felt supported enough to keep experimenting with different ways of moving horses that would loosen and relax them.

■ A Pioneering Paradigm Shift

I met Sally Swift in 1981, and Linda Tellington-Jones, creator of the Tellington Method®, in 1986. These pioneering horsewomen were shifting the prevailing paradigm of the horse-rider relationship from what I call "cramming and jamming" to a new model of horsemanship. I was ecstatic to find such kindred spirits who worked with horses out of knowledge and balance rather than fear and force.

From Sally I learned body awareness and alignment, and she reinforced my belief that the rider needs to learn how to feel the horse through her body. In order for this to happen, I knew that the horse had

The Feldenkrais Method®

Does your back hurt? Do you have trouble focusing your attention? Have you stopped participating in activities you used to enjoy? The Feldenkrais Method is for anyone who wants to reconnect with their natural abilities to move, think, and feel. Whether you want to be more comfortable sitting at your computer, playing with your children and grandchildren, or performing a favorite pastime, these gentle lessons can improve your overall well-being. Learning to move with less effort makes daily life easier. Because the Feldenkrais Method focuses on the relationship between movement and thought, increased mental awareness and creativity accompany physical improvements.

—From *The Feldenkrais Method of Somatic Education* (www.feldenkrais.com)

to be able to deliver movement and motion to his rider. Sally introduced me to the Alexander Technique, a method that helps people align their body, lengthen their spine, and rid themselves of harmful tension (see sidebar, p. xiv).

With Linda I discovered a whole new way of looking at horses from the ground. And eventually I realized that horses and people of all disciplines, both competitors and recreational riders, had the same body issues and bracing patterns. Such habitual patterns of holding and tension had to be released before horse and rider could truly move with freedom and self-carriage—what dressage riders call "throughness." This signifies the energy from the horse's hind legs moving up and through the rider's body and back again to the horse in a complete cycle of reciprocal motion.

Linda introduced me to the Feldenkrais Method™, which also shaped my understanding of movement in horse and human bodies through the concept of learning by doing subtle, nonhabitual exercises. These exercises allow the nervous system to release tension and discomfort, paving the way for new learning (see sidebar above).

▌How Recognizing a Disconnect Led to the Ultimate Connection

Making the shift away from my traditional equestrian training was not an easy path. All my life I'd heard the rhetoric of softness and "throughness," but I wasn't seeing it in action. I did not feel it in my own body or in my horse's body. But everyone around me—my peers and colleagues—just kept riding as if working harder would solve every problem.

Once I knew there was a major "disconnect" between what was being written about riding and what was happening to horses as a result of being ridden, I allowed myself to be creative with all of the "stuck" horses I encountered. Each one of these animals gave me new challenges to figure out—how to create more ease and elasticity in their body from their work, instead of taking it away. Slowly, over a period of many years, my groundwork techniques started to take form in ways I had never imagined. It was interesting when I first introduced this groundwork in my clinics how skeptical people were—mainly because they did not yet understand its relationship to riding. Some were still convinced you had to "fix the horse under saddle," not realizing how much more they could receive and give to their horse if they truly *connected* with his body from the ground *first*.

King lost his stride because he was compressed and shut down. Slowly I started learning that every horse that came to me with "bad habits" was the result of being ridden on the forehand and further compressed with "gadgets." None of this was necessary. I had to figure out a way to teach people to do it differently and discover the freedom that comes from letting go of bracing, compression, and tightness. Thirty years after I learned how to influence King's way of going without even sitting on him, Connected Groundwork and Connected Riding are my answers to this universal riding dilemma.

I invite you to use this book as a learning manual and reference guide for Connected Groundwork exercises. What you're about to read is a technical manual, very dense in detail. Take it slowly, *play* with the exercises with curiosity, as well as a sense of wonder and discovery, and you will be pleased with what awaits you.

Where to Begin

I suggest the following steps for those new to Connected Groundwork and Connected Riding—in essence, you should "sample" different parts of the book rather than read it straight through:

1   Read Part I to understand the context of this approach and familiarize yourself with the terminology related to my methods. Then thumb through the exercises to acquaint yourself with them.

2   Next, experiment with the simplest groundwork maneuvers, such as the first five standing-still exercises—Part IV: Beginning Exercises for the Horse (p. 57), from *Cheek Press* through *Chin Rest*. Think of the first part of this process as finding your dance rhythm to new music. "Play" with the exercises—it is easier and more beneficial to stay relaxed and curious as you observe how you and your horse interact. This will prove more fruitful than trying to get the exercise "done correctly." As you and your horse become more at ease with each exercise, proficiency will naturally develop. You will become increasingly more aware of where to touch the horse and how to move him when he "gets stuck" or loses momentum.

3   Build an understanding of the basic elements of Connected Groundwork, including *Slide Up, Slide Out* and *Draw the Bow* (p. 49), and *Combing the Line* (p. 51).

4   Once you have gotten a feel for the groundwork at a standstill, go to *Walking "S" One Hand* (p. 102). As discussed in Part II: Exercises for the Handler (p. 19), begin cultivating an awareness of your own body, making sure your wrists aren't bent, your back and hips aren't locked, and you are in *Neutral Posture* (p. 20).

5   Experiment for 10 to 15 minutes each day before you ride (and on days you don't ride). Once you have developed a groundwork routine that seems right for you and your horse, spend up to 30 minutes on it each day before getting on your horse and noticing its effects. Eventually you can effectively use the groundwork to prepare your horse for riding.

Where You Are Headed

The scope of this book is from "head to tail"—for both you and your horse. As you gain awareness of the "segments" of human and equine bodies, and begin to understand how to create and recreate elasticity and freedom of movement, you will be ready and able to begin "dancing with your horse" on the ground in more complex exercises. The final piece in this book is the crown jewel, the "workhorse" of the basic Connected Groundwork method: *Connected Longeing* (p. 119). This is where all the moving segments come together in concert to prepare you and the horse for riding—rebalancing from the ground, in sync, together.

Case Studies

Throughout this book I have included Case Studies with before-and-after photographs, chosen from horses and riders around the world who have experienced the positive impact of Connected Groundwork. These are wonderful, yet "ordinary," riding and driving horses that presented challenges due to their conformation, previous training issues, or both.

Among the consistently observed results reported: improved muscling and strength to better carry their own and their rider's weight; happier, more cooperative, and focused attitudes; and becoming "unstuck"—softening, lightening, and "releasing" (see p. 8). These Case Studies are dynamic proof that horses can improve their way of going, shift their weight off the forehand, and with consistent support from the ground, become a joy to ride and be around. As one rider wrote us, "Connected Groundwork has given me my horse back! I now feel like I have the connection with my horse that I always dreamed of, and this is just the beginning!"

Note: Throughout this book, for simplicity riders and handlers are referred as "she"; most horses are referred to as "he."

PART I

Introduction to Connected Groundwork

WHAT YOU NEED TO KNOW BEFORE YOU BEGIN

The Language of Connected Groundwork

Before you begin to practice the exercises in this book, it is helpful if you understand the language and core principles of Connected Groundwork (some, although not all, apply to Connected Riding as well). These concepts are applied throughout all the work, whether with the human or the equine body.

Learning to do Connected Groundwork with your horse is like learning a new language of horsemanship. Through my years of teaching, the language and imagery of my approach has evolved in order to give my students a somatic sense of what is happening in their body, and in their horse's body, as they practice the exercises. Over time you will begin putting the "words" and "phrases" that follow together into coherent "sentences." The language may be a bit mind-boggling in the beginning, but stick with it. Once you experience connection on a line with your horse, you'll be hooked—and on your way to a more fulfilling partnership with your horse.

BASE DOWN/BASE UP For a horse to have freedom of movement, his "base" has to go up and down with every stride. When the horse is *base down*, his movement is inhibited and his spine is compressed. The neck is retracted and the horse is on the forehand. He can only pull himself along with his front feet (fig. 1.1 A). When the horse is *base up*, he can use his back and hindquarters more efficiently and with less fatigue. The neck "telescopes" (see p. 9), the withers and back lift, and the hind legs can propel him forward (fig. 1.1 B).

BREATHING FROM YOUR BELLY (ABDOMINAL BREATHING) This is the most efficient way for the rider/handler to maximize air intake into the lungs. When inhaling, the diaphragm is pulled down, the abdomen expands, and the lungs fill with air. This action expands the rib cage in all directions and is felt all the way into the armpits as the lower back fills. The movement at the back of the rib cage lightens your body and releases stress; it allows your joints to move in freedom, lengthening your spine. This breathing pattern is easiest when your body is in **Neutral Posture** (see p. 6).

BRACING Involuntary habitual patterns created in horse and human when muscles rigidly tighten and joints lock against movement. Bracing patterns lead to

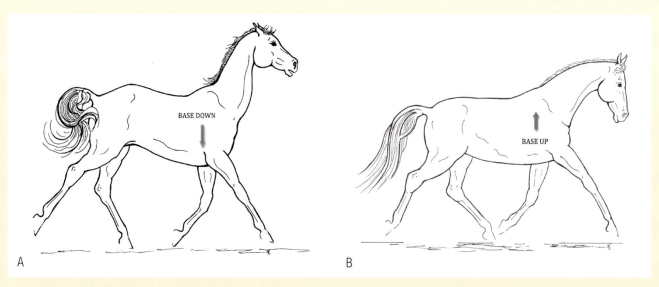

1.1 A & B Drawing A depicts a horse *base down*: The withers are dropped, the horse is retracting his neck, and he is on the forehand. Drawing B shows a horse *base up*: He is lifting his withers and "telescoping" his neck (see p. 9).

1.2 This six-year-old Andalusian stallion and his rider volunteered for one of my demos in Spain. At the beginning of the session, the horse was in a false frame (see p. 4 to see the "before" photo) and the rider remarked that the horse felt lazy. After I worked with the rider, the horse completely changed his posture and attitude. In this photo he is connected and *coming through, base up* with his neck *"telescoped"* and his back lifted. He is moving freely forward and is very light and energetic in the rider's hands.

1.3 A & B Connection, such as that exhibited here between me and this horse, is described by many as a magical feeling (A). You'll learn to recognize its characteristics through the exercises in this book. The five-year-old Arab shown in B was barely started under saddle at the time of this photo, and yet here he is learning how to stretch into contact. He is focused and reciprocating (p. 8). His owner can feel the energy generated by his hind legs in her hands. (Much to the chagrin of his owner, a yearling colt had eaten this horse's tail!)

compression, imbalance, and discomfort or pain, and are responsible for much of the disharmony between a horse and his handler/rider. Connected Groundwork releases such bracing patterns so horse and human are free to move in **self-carriage** (see p. 8).

COMBING THE LINE A movement in Connected Groundwork when each of your hands alternately reaches up in turn to the horse's halter and "combs" down the lead line toward your body in a smooth, continuous motion. The line runs between your thumb (on top) and the index and middle fingers. Your elbows have a soft bend—they are not locked. The combing motion provides a steady oscillating rhythm to the horse, encouraging him to reach into contact with you and **"telescope"** (see p. 9) his neck forward and down, thereby encouraging his "base" to come up (see p. 2). The combing action

helps break up tension, and it is also useful while mounted to prevent barging and bracing patterns, as well as pulling on the reins.

COMING THROUGH This term is used to describe the feeling of a horse—in-hand or under saddle—when the energy of his hind legs transfers a sensation of power through his body and into your hands. "Coming through" also refers to the motion of the horse when the hind legs are creating enough energy to stretch the horse's topline and create a balanced, forward-moving stride that appears and feels light and effortless (fig. 1.2).

CONNECTION This is the ultimate state of partnership in which neither horse nor handler is tense or braced in any part of their body; in which the horse is moving fluidly, softly, and lightly, dynamically expanding in every direction; and in which the horse **reciprocates** (see p. 8), maintaining a bungee-like connection on the line or rein. Often described as a "magical" sensation, when you and your horse are *connected* you can feel the energy of your horse's hind legs "in your hands" as his neck **"telescopes"** (see p. 9) and the line or reins feel "alive."

"DEAD WEIGHT" AND "LIVE WEIGHT" When you are "dead weight" to your horse, your bones and joints don't have freedom to move. For example, if you arch your back while leading a horse with contact on the line, the horse feels that you are pulling on him. There is no give and take, **oscillations** (see p. 6), or "buoy" in your body; you are compressing all the elasticity available.

"Live weight" is when you are in **Neutral Posture** (see p. 6); every joint and bone in the horse's body has freedom to move. If you have contact on the line the horse feels the elastic connection supporting and going with him as he moves. Your joints aren't stiff, nor is your upper body falling behind the motion or forcing the motion.

ENGAGING This is building the power and "priming the pump" to activate core muscles and generate workable energy. Engaging involves a lengthening of the horse's topline. (Neither horse nor human can engage with a tight back.) When you throw an inflated ball down to the ground, it will come up again. It has buoyancy and elasticity. It is this buoyancy and elasticity that makes engagement—and thus the ability to repeat each stride without additional stress—possible. For example, when you *Walk an S* (see p. 102) and feel the horse's hind end start to **come through** (see p. 3), or when you can feel the connection and release in your hand and the energy of the walk pick up, *that* is the beginning of engagement. It is the result of the activation of reciprocal energy (see also Cycle of Connection, p. 11)

EQUAL AND OPPOSING Based on Newton's Third Law of Physics, every *action* has a *reaction*, equal in magnitude and opposite in direction. This principle is exemplified by what happens when we step off a boat onto the bank of a lake: As we move in the direction of the shore, the boat tends to move off in the opposite direction (leaving us facedown in the water if we aren't

1.4 Here you can see the habitual way this six-year-old Andalusian was "put on the bit"—a "false frame" that is behind the vertical and overbent, resulting in him being base down (p. 2) and strung out behind. Notice that the rider's back is braced. I worked on the rider's body, and after a brief session, this horse completely changed his posture and "came through" (see "after" photo on p. 3).

careful!) When we learn to acknowledge this universal law in our work with horses, whether on the ground or in the saddle, we discover a way of finding **connection** (see p. 3) without pulling, bracing, or tugging. If you brace in *your* body while riding or working on the ground, your horse will correspondingly brace in *his* body. If you lean behind the vertical when you ride, your horse will be on the forehand. And so on.

FALSE FRAME (FORCED FRAME) This human-made phenomenon is created by force and the bracing patterns of a horse's rider/handler. A "false frame" occurs when a horse travels with his head "held" by the rider's hands so the poll is not allowed to release freely with each stride (fig. 1.4). When ridden this way, the horse's back and sides are also squeezed and braced against the rider's body. The base of the horse's neck and withers cannot rise, limiting range of motion and making it difficult for the hind legs to track up or come under the horse's torso, or for the back to lift. In this posture, the horse cannot carry himself or a rider well or efficiently because he remains braced on the forehand. Training gadgets such as side-reins and martingales contribute to this compressive posture.

"HEAVY" AND "LIGHT" Sometimes, even when you are in a Connected Groundwork leading position, the horse's head will feel like a ton of bricks—as in "heavy." It can make your arm feel like bracing back, but you have to stay soft by **Meeting and Melting** (see below). Heavy horses are often locked in the atlas area of the poll, as well as the upper neck vertebrae through the shoulder. The heaviness you feel is a combination of the bracing and tension of the muscles. Heavier built breeds, such as draft mixes, have a propensity for tension and bracing on the forehand as they are built more for pulling than for riding.

You want your horse to feel "light" in your hands. But light also has to have a solid grounding; it isn't weightlessness you are after. Imagine holding a tennis ball in one hand and tossing it a foot up in the air. When it comes back into your hand, it will have a light yet solid feeling. Toss up a ping-pong ball and it may not return to your hand as its relative weightlessness may cause it to drift. And tossing and catching a bowling ball would be almost impossible. Lightness has just the right balance—a reciprocity that is receivable.

INSIDE AND OUTSIDE While doing Connected Groundwork, if you are standing on the left side of the horse, tracking to the left, the horse's *inside* hind leg is the left one and the *outside* hind leg is the right one. *Inside* is the near (left) side when you are standing on the left; *outside* is the offside.

MEET AND MELT When working with horses, a common reaction on the human's part is to offer resistance or pull back when a horse pulls, jerks, or gets **heavy** (see above). The concept of *Meet and Melt* is a way of changing this automatic response (the opposition reflex) into a conscious habit where you *Meet* (match) the pressure of the horse on the other end of the line and then slowly *Melt* (release) the muscles that you used to match the pressure (fig. 1.5). The result overrides your tendency to pull and hang on your horse, and thus prevents the horse pulling and bracing in return. The slow *Melt* allows

1.5 To experience *Meet and Melt*, hook your index fingers together as shown here, stretching both elbows out to the sides and holding your fingers in the middle of your sternum. You will feel a strong connection in both hands. Both elbows are *equal and opposing* (see p. 4), carrying out the same action/reaction in opposite directions. When you slowly soften one arm, you will notice that the other arm automatically follows—*Melting* exactly the same amount and at the same time. This principle works the same way with your horse, whether you are holding a lead rope, line, or reins. What is remarkable about this process is that you are using your arm—not your hand—to create a dynamic connection. To an outside observer it appears as if your arm does not move. What is important to realize is the almost magical result: You can change pulling, bracing, heaviness, and stiffness in a horse, and allow the horse to rebalance—without effort.

the horse time to rebalance and soften. So, *Meeting* is an invitation and *Melting* is **reciprocation** and **release** (see p. 8). The concepts of **equal and opposing** (see p. 4) and *Meeting and Melting* create dynamic connection and reciprocity—both parties carry responsibility for their body position (see also **Long Stretch Slow Give**, p. 6).

LONG STRETCH SLOW GIVE When you do **Meet and Melt** (see above) in an alternating, repeating cycle with rhythm (one arm and then the other—although you can choose to do just one side whenever you need to) it becomes *Long Stretch Slow Give*. The easiest way to begin is by saying to yourself as you go through the steps of *Meet and Melt*, "Meet, 1-2-3-4, Melt, 1-2-3-4-5-6-7-8." Another combination is, "Meet, 1-2-3-4, Hold, 1-2-3-4, Melt, 1-2-3-4-5-6-7-8." The idea is to *give* more than you *take*, and to take back with a soft hand and straight wrist. You should engage the upper arm and shoulder muscles on the *Meet* and soften when you *Melt*.

NEUTRAL POSTURE (NEUTRAL PELVIS) is your center point, whether you are sitting, standing, walking, or riding. A neutral place is not fixed but dynamic. It's the posture you return to, from where all balance and connection comes. When you are in neutral posture, your pelvis is neither tipped forward nor backward; it rests on the middle of the seat bones (*ischial tuberosity*) when you are sitting. When your back is arched and your chest slightly lifted, the pelvis tips forward. When your back is slumped and the chest slightly collapsed, the pelvis tips backward. *Neutral Posture* signifies that the sternum and sacrum are parallel to each other, and it is the only posture where the body can experience pain-free movement and dynamic expansion (fig. 1.6).

If you *are not* in neutral, the horse has to compensate for your imbalance and instability by **bracing** (see p. 3) or counterbalancing. When your pelvis *is* in neutral, your upper body "buoys" itself as your core muscles automatically engage to rebalance your body as necessary—so the horse doesn't have to compensate for you (see fig. 1.7). In *Neutral Posture*, each hip joint is free to move, allowing each leg to move independently. When sitting or standing in neutral, the body is most stable, strong, and "free" so the limbs can be used effectively without restriction. This is the place of the **self-carriage** I speak of for horses (see p. 8) and humans and the optimal posture for all of your daily activities. (For more about how to find *Neutral Posture/ Pelvis,* see Part II: Exercises for the Handler, p. 19.)

OPENING THE RIB CAGE During **abdominal "belly"**

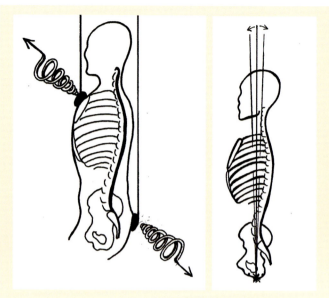

1.6 Here you see *Neutral Posture*, with the sternum (upper left) and sacrum (lower right) parallel to each other.

1.7 *Neutral Posture* allows your upper body to "buoy" itself (move slightly as necessary) in order to rebalance and keep you stable without bracing.

breathing (see p. 2), as the sternum and the sacrum move away from each other, the sternum moves *forward and up* while the sacrum moves *backward and down*, allowing the back to lengthen and the rib cage to expand.

OSCILLATING RHYTHM *Oscillation* is the invisible, repetitive rhythm the horse's body receives from the handler when she walks in *Neutral Posture* while touching the horse, or leading or working with him on a line (see p. 37). This rhythm overrides tension and invites the horse to reciprocate.

In *Neutral Posture*, both sides of your body—and your horse's body—are independent and free to move. When the horse receives the rhythm of the movement of your feet through the line, through your hand at the halter or anywhere else on his body, or through your seat bones in the saddle, this produces what we call *Oscillating Rhythm*. It's like dancing, where two beings are synchronized in movement from side to side, front to back, and up to down. This creates **live weight** (see p. 4) in you and lightness, reciprocity, and elasticity in you and the horse. When you are not, or your horse is not, moving with *Oscillating Rhythm*, the result is stiffness, compression, and bracing. If you are not in *Neutral Posture* you have no *Oscillating Rhythm* and the horse experiences you as **dead weight** (see p. 4).

OUT OF BALANCE In a stressful situation, if your handling adds tension or imbalance to the horse or if he already exhibits poor posture, his natural instincts of "Fight, Flight, Freeze, Faint, or Fidget" (as identified by Linda Tellington-Jones in the Tellington Method—see recommended resources on p. 137) will be amplified. Connected Groundwork gives you tools with which you can rebalance the out-of-balance horse and reinstate focus and calmness. These tools provide clear boundaries without the use of force, fear, or pain.

"OWNING" YOUR ELBOWS In order to keep the slack out of the line or reins without tensing or bracing the body, the handler or rider's elbows must stretch backward in an almost invisible movement. This continuous reciprocal process maintains the handler/rider's dynamic arm connection to the horse's head or mouth. *"Owning" your elbows* engages the muscles in the upper arms and shoulders in a soft isometric contact that is continually readjusted to maintain supportive contact on the line or reins. This is only achieved when your body is in **Neutral Posture** (see p. 6), which allows the core muscles of your body to spontaneously engage in response to the amount of support the horse needs at any given moment. When you are in *neutral*, your horse feels your contact as *supporting* rather than *pulling*.

Note: When doing groundwork, the bend in your elbow may be more open than it would be when you are riding. "Owning" simply means engaging the upper arm muscles to establish a connection—it does not always mean your arms must be bent and held beside your torso.

PLUMB LINE / "BUOYING" The *plumb line* is the true vertical line perpendicular to the ground, which passes through the handler or rider's ear, shoulder, hip, and ankle. Just like horses, handlers and riders can be ahead,

behind, or "on the vertical." In most instances, humans are behind the vertical, whether riding or standing.

When a handler/rider is standing or sitting in **Neutral Posture** and **breathing abdominally** (see pp. 6 and 2), her body has the ability to freely "buoy" back and forth across the plumb line with each breath (fig. 1.7). This buoying motion is a minute rebalancing movement (think of a buoy bobbing on a wave) of the upper body over the hips. When a horse feels this rebalancing from your body, he buoys and rebalances, too. When you are in *Neutral Posture*, your upper body automatically buoys with each stride that you take. When you are *not* in neutral, your body doesn't buoy across the plumb line; it stays behind the vertical and becomes a drag on you and your horse.

PROCESSING The horse needs time to integrate new information into his nervous system. When *processing*, the horse is in an obvious semi-conscious, sleepy, or alpha-like state: the eyelids close; the lips quiver; the horse yawns, licks, and chews; or the horse just seems to be deeply absorbed in some sort of inward concentration. This can last from a few seconds to a few minutes. You will know when the horse is finished as he will blink and appear to wake up or something will capture his attention.

While practicing a specific groundwork exercise (especially if you are having trouble), stop doing the exercise for a minute or two, and allow the horse to process the information (fig. 1.8). He will take a huge breath, or begin licking and chewing as he lowers his head and neck. This demonstrates he has integrated the work into his nervous system. When you return to the exercise you may find the horse to be much more peaceful and tuned in to you.

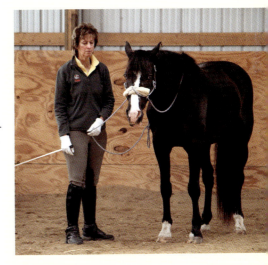

1.8 A horse allowed to process a new lesson appears deeply absorbed for a few seconds to a few minutes. Often, the handler goes into a similar state!

REBALANCING This is the final phase in the *Cycle of Connection* (see p. 11). Your horse must do it again and again: *re*release, *re*engage, and *re*balance in each stride, with all four feet. When your horse is connected and rebalancing, you will observe a fluid continuity of motion, from head to tail and back again.

RELEASING *Releasing* is the word I use to describe the conscious act of the handler or rider to soften and let go of tension in the lower back, wrists, knees, hips, and shoulders. It also describes the sensation of the horse letting go of tension and softening to your touch or **reciprocating** and **"telescoping"** his neck (see below and p. 9).

Releasing in the human involves an expansion and lengthening in the spine as well as between the sternum and sacrum, essentially lengthening the body. Similarly, the horse lengthens between the front legs and the top of his croup. The "release" looks like a dry sponge immersed in water—it slowly expands. (For more on releasing, see the *Cycle of Connection* on p. 11.)

RECIPROCITY As the horse assimilates Connected Groundwork into his body, he returns the connection you offer through his active participation. You give the horse rhythm and support from your body—and the horse *reciprocates* by **"telescoping"** his neck (see p. 9), stretching his topline, and engaging from behind. You may feel the energy and rhythm of his hind legs coming through into your hands. Reciprocity is positive reinforcement for the work you will be doing: for example, when you *Slide Out* on the line (see p. 49) and feel the horse take up a light, consistent contact instead of falling away from the contact or becoming heavy in your hand.

ROTATION The ability to swivel (not tip or twist) your torso in order to maintain a smooth, unbroken connection with your horse is called *rotation*. This is the foundation for changing direction, moving laterally, and creating bend and straightness in the horse during both groundwork and ridden work. Imagine your upper torso turning from deep inside the core, just below the sternum. This spiral movement allows you to stay in **Neutral Posture** (see p. 6) and leverages your core strength, which directs the horse's movements, releases tension, overrides bracing, assists in rebalancing, and encourages lengthening of the horse's spine.

To ensure rotation and prevent twisting, your body must be in *Neutral Posture* with your lower back "full" and soft. There cannot be tightening in and around the spine or rib cage. During rotation, your shoulders and hips remain parallel to the ground; your head and shoulders turn in a different direction from your legs and hips; and your body turns around its own vertical axis. This can only happen if you allow your core muscles to work and your back and chest muscles to stay soft.

SELF-CARRIAGE This term refers to the horse's ideal posture during movement: The horse continuously releases at the poll, lifts his withers and the base of his neck, pushes with both hind legs, and freely rebalances himself during each stride. The horse is able to shift his weight from front to back, back to front, side to side, and down to up in a dynamic process. As the horse moves, the "push" of the hind legs comes up through the horse and (when applicable) the rider's body (see my description of the cycle through the handler's body on p. 11). This energy travels through the rider to the front of the horse, then back through the rider to the hind end of the horse—it's a continuous cycle of rebalancing and reciprocity of motion and energy. As the ability to self-carry is developed, the horse is able to maintain balance and freedom for longer periods of time, and the adjustments required to maintain this posture become minimal.

SOFTENING A shift from tension, rigidity, or stiffness to a yielding state is called *softening*. It is often accompanied by a noticeable exhalation of breath. When doing Connected Groundwork exercises such as *Cheek Press* (p. 58) or *Chin Rest* (p. 69), your hands support the horse, allowing him to soften. In addition to the horse's muscles softening beneath your hands, you may also notice a postural change—i.e., from a high head to a lowered head. You may also sense your own body softening, especially if you have been tightening your hip joints or back. Be aware of this; your horse can't soften unless you do, too!

1.9 When a horse is asked to change direction, he may plant his feet and appear "stuck" until he figures out how to shift his weight more efficiently.

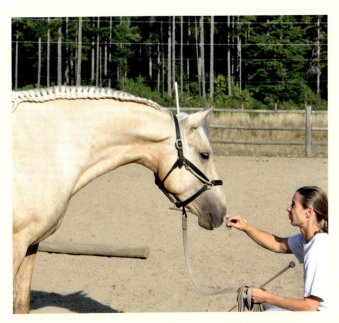

1.10 This is a lovely example of a horse "telescoping" his neck forward from its base.

STUCK In this book "stuck" refers to a horse that plants his feet, stops moving, or appears unable to move a specific foot when asked (fig. 1.9). The situation is remedied by allowing the horse to stand and do nothing for a minute or two, and then simplifying the request that was made or "going for walk" (see p. 59).

TELESCOPING This is a desirable response in which the horse "lets go" at the poll and extends his neck out and forward from the base as it moves upward with each stride (fig. 1.10). In contrast, when a horse goes behind the bridle or "sucks back," the base of the neck is down, the neck contracts and compresses, and movement in the poll is constricted.

THINKING "UP" THROUGH THE WRIST The process of remaining light in your forearm and staying straight through the wrist as contact is made on the horse's halter or when working him on the line is called *thinking "up" through the wrist*. This practice keeps the horse light, soft, and supported. It is the act of engaging the forearm muscles to prevent the forearm from becoming "**dead weight**" (see p. 4) or being rendered ineffective by being moved forward out of position by the horse. It prevents bending at the wrist, which takes away the elasticity from every joint in your body, inviting bracing and heavy hands.

▌ All about Connection

Having come from a strong Centered Riding tradition, I found it necessary to clearly differentiate the essence of my work as an evolution of Sally Swift's contributions. "Centering" oneself is certainly one aspect of connection. However, as my research and knowledge developed, I knew there were more pieces to the puzzle of connecting horse and rider. I realized that the process of connection begins from the ground by reeducating horse and human posture. Once posture is free and "neutral" (see p. 20), it allows the movement of the horse to come from his hind end through the rider and

A Holistic Approach to Horsemanship

A holistic approach is a part of Connected Riding and its values, which are outlined here:

SAFETY
▸ Promote self-awareness and self-responsibility.
▸ Nurture respect for individual differences and learning processes.
▸ Encourage, physical, mental, and emotional well-being.

EMPOWERMENT
▸ Support self-exploration, personal growth, discovery, and mastery (see below).

KINSHIP
▸ Cultivate teamwork, cooperation, and responsibility to a group and to a win-win process.

MASTERY
▸ Confirm ownership and integration of skills.
▸ Challenge teachers and students to reach their full potential.
▸ Engender creativity.
▸ Share knowledge with others.

back through the horse in a cycle (see more about this on p. 11). I named this method to convey the totality of this connection process.

"Connection," in my lexicon, describes the all-important horse-and-human dynamic that enables physical, emotional, and mental balance to occur in both beings. When the horse "connects" to his core muscles, hind feet, and poll, he can lift his back, balance, and rebalance himself readily and in all directions. Balance can only happen with connection. The role of the human, whether handling the horse from the ground or riding on his back, is to facilitate connection that supports the horse so he can rebalance himself with each stride.

▌ Cornerstones of Connected Groundwork

In the world of riding instruction, one frequently hears words such as *self-carriage, coming through, collection, lightness,* and *bascule* (lifting of the back). They all describe universal goals of riding: to capture the energy that originates in the horse's haunches, to transfer the weight from his forehand to his hindquarters, and to recreate under saddle the freedom of motion evident in the horse at liberty.

While most riders agree that these goals are admirable, achieving them requires more than paying homage to words; success requires attention to their meanings in action. Our horses are often unwitting victims of a communication gap. They are most often willing and eager to please, but their path to progress is hampered, even shut down, by a lack of congruence in their human counterparts' thoughts and actions.

In actuality, many horses become stiffer by the year despite the best intentions of their handlers. Many riders unintentionally contribute to their horse's bracing patterns. You see, horses are more often ridden in a state of compression, bracing, and tension rather than ease, lightness, and what I call "connection" (and what others often call *self-carriage*—see p. 8—a good term, if often misunderstood).

However, by making subtle—yet powerful—changes in the way riders use their body when they ride and handle horses, they can intervene in this cycle of stiffness and regain their horse's suppleness. Such changes completely shift the way horses move, learn, and respond.

With Connected Groundwork, bracing patterns in horse and human can be substantially diminished, opening a multitude of possibilities and choices for both handler and horse. It is a dynamic in which a horse is free to shift weight with ease; move by letting go of tension instead of getting tense to move; and lengthen in the body rather than compress. Without this, you sacrifice freedom of motion, elasticity, focus, and the horse's ability to participate in his response (what I call *reciprocity,* see p. 8).

1.11 Connection in motion: This seven-year-old child is walking her 34-year-old horse in connection.

Hallmarks of Connection

The horse transforms from:
▸ Bracing to releasing and relaxing
▸ Compressing to expanding
▸ Unyielding to softening and giving
▸ Moving stiffly and mechanically to moving fluidly in every direction
▸ Moving in a "false frame" to engaging and coiling the lumbosacral joint
▸ Heavy on the forehand to light on the forehand, lifting at the base of the neck
▸ Evading to participating
▸ Failing to respond to willing and focused
▸ Overreacting to responding in a quiet, confident manner

▌ The Cycle of Connection

As the horse moves, the energy created by the hind legs travels through the horse's back and neck, then through the halter and line to the handler. In the handler, the energy from the horse travels through the arms, down the back to the feet, and is reciprocated from the feet back up through her body to the horse (fig. 1.11). The handler must be in Neutral Posture for this to occur. The cycle repeats with every stride. (The cycle is similar when you are riding: As the horse moves, the "push" of the hind legs comes up through the horse and the rider's body, to the front of the horse, then back through the rider to the hind end of the horse.)

When the horse moves freely without bracing, the poll moves slightly with each stride, the back and withers lift, the hind legs push, and the tail swings gently. The energy initiates in the hindquarters. From tail to poll, you see a rhythmic, oscillating movement from back to front and front to back, rippling through the spine like a caterpillar in motion. It is a pattern of continuous releasing and reengaging. The topline comes together like an accordion, then

expands like a well-syncopated melody. With each stride the horse builds power, gathering the hind end and producing more loft and bascule. The dynamic of loin coiling and expansion equals release.

The Cycle of Connection is comprised of:

→ **Releasing (see also p. 8)**—signs that a horse is letting go of tension or stress—are a joy to observe. They include licking; chewing; deep breathing; yawning; softening of the eyes or expression; blowing through the nostrils, flaring the nostrils, relaxing the mouth and chin; and lowering the head, poll, and neck (figs. 1.12 A & B). In addition, the base of neck softens, the horse is able to stop and start easily, and he can change direction without stiffening, bracing, or altering speed or tempo. The horse is *with* you, relaxed and focused.

→ **Engaging/reengaging (see also p. 4)** is the stride by stride coiling of the loins and lumbosacral (LS) joint that creates the kinetic energy that is translated into forward motion. The neck stretches ("telescopes"), the back comes up, the spine gets longer, the core muscles of the belly engage, and the hind legs reach further under the horse. A horse has to

1.12 A & B Signs that a horse is releasing chronic patterns of bracing and tension include softening of the eyes or expression, blowing and flaring of the nostrils, and relaxing the mouth and chin.

engage in this way to balance, rebalance, and stay in connection. A horse in self-carriage is not a frozen, rigid form in a "false frame" (see p. 4): When worked or ridden in a connected way, he is like an elastic bungee cord, lengthening and shortening in multiple dimensions.

→ Rebalancing (see also p. 8) is the final phase in the cycle of connected movement. As I mentioned earlier, your horse must do it again and again: *re*release, *re*engage, and *re*balance in each stride, with all four feet. When your horse is connected, you will observe a fluid continuity of motion, from tail to head and back again.

The Cycle of Disconnection

During *dis*connection—moments of tension or falling out of balance—horses and humans instinctively brace their body. When two beings move together while both bracing, they lose their elasticity and ability to rebalance. The horse's quality of movement, willingness, and desire to cooperate slip away. When balance is lost, more evasions and training "issues"—such as spooking, tripping, rearing, bolting, balking, and running through the bridle—take place. Instead of focusing on stopping

The Benefits of Rebalancing Your Horse

"The eye of the master maketh of the horse."
—Xenophon

We know that most horses, when standing, place more weight on the forehand—this is how they are designed. And through the centuries that horses have been ridden they have, for the most part, remained on the forehand. When a horse is on the forehand, his movement is compressed and limited. Beginning with Xenophon, masters of horsemanship have explored ways of creating more out of the movements that horses offer. They have also studied the changes that occur in the horse's body and his movement when he is ridden. By working your horse from the ground in preparation for riding, you have a unique opportunity to lay the foundation for a horse that finds being ridden an easy and comfortable experience. You will help your horse learn to rebalance his weight in movement, as if shifting to "rear-wheel drive." In order to maximize your horse's natural elevation of movement under saddle, he must relearn how to be efficient in motion while carrying weight on his back. This requires the horse to:

▸ Access all *Four Corners* (see p. 114), use both sides of his body, and move each leg independently
▸ Transition from gait to gait with ease
▸ Lift the base of the neck and engage the hindquarters

the evasion from occurring, which is only a symptom of a deeper imbalance, working on improving the horse's posture and engagement opens the door to balance and harmony—the essence of connection (figs. 1.13 A & B and 1.14 A & B).

When habitual bracing patterns take hold, a group of muscles clump together and remain contracted, losing their capacity for freedom of movement. Then fibrous, connective tissue surrounding the muscles (known as *fascia*) adheres to bone or other fascia, causing further restriction. Such muscle tightness

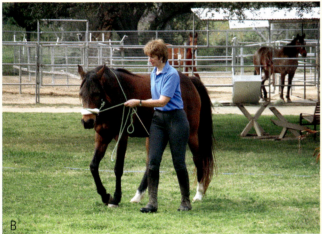

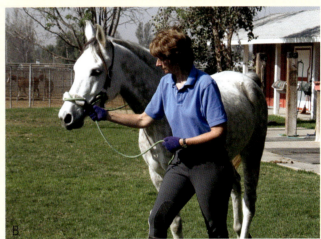

1.13 A & B Disconnected (A): When this mare fell out of balance, her pattern was to twist her head. Connected (B): After doing a few Connected Groundwork exercises, this mare was totally focused and quiet.

1.14 A & B Disconnected (A): When a horse tilts his head while turning as shown here, he is compensating for tension in his head and neck. Connected (B): Here the horse is beginning to soften and focus, allowing his head and neck to progressively lower.

places undue pressure on the skeletal system of the horse—bones move out of alignment, tension increases, and movement cannot flow freely through the body. Chances are the handler is pretty tense when the horse is out of balance, so *to change the horse, the human must change first.*

An out-of-balance posture keeps a horse "stuck" on the forehand (see sidebar, p. 12) and unable to shift his

weight efficiently. In the face of such imbalances, drilling with coercive or repetitive training methods, especially with "gadgets" such as martingales and draw reins, forces horses into more compression and a "false frame."

In addition, the popular technique of flexing a horse's head and neck repeatedly in both directions places undue strain and compression on the neck and prevents the horse from "telescoping" his neck, reaching for

Observe Your Horse's Patterns of Imbalance and Disconnection

All horses have patterns of disconnection. It is beneficial to become familiar with how and when your horse disconnects and loses his balance. From the first steps of leading, to work on the line and then under saddle, the same patterns prevail. The more you help your horse learn how to rebalance himself when an imbalance occurs, the more quickly he will develop his rebalancing response. By practicing the Connected Groundwork exercises you affirm a posture in your horse that strengthens his balance and self-carriage.

  This series of photos depicts a young Arab mare named Perle who displayed extreme tension, reactivity, and bracing patterns during her first Connected Groundwork sessions (figs. 1.15 A–F). She was believed to have an underlying physical issue involving her temporomandibular joint (TMJ), as well as dental problems. (Eventually these issues were resolved, and the mare went on to complete several distance rides.) Studying your horse's movements and reactions as we study Perle's here is one of the first steps to changing the Cycle of Disconnection to a Cycle of Connection.

Photo A Perle sticks her head out and grinds her teeth, indicating discomfort in the "hinges" of her head, poll, and neck. As a horse

becomes "connected," these behaviors are greatly lessened or disappear altogether.

Photo B Twisting the head (as Perle is doing here) is a symptom of disconnection horses exhibit when there is tension in their head and neck. Such horses have difficulty rotating and releasing their head and neck during changes of direction.

Photo C When a horse tosses or twirls his head, or pulls in any way, I let the line slide through my fingers (see more about handling the Connected Groundwork line on p. 49).

Photo D Working on one line to the left, Perle is heavy on the forehand, unbalanced, and disconnected, with her head tilted in toward the handler.

Photo E To the right, Perle tosses her head up and disconnects on the line. Most people would see this as an evasion; however, the mare is trying to communicate her imbalance. If a horse exhibits these behaviors for more than a few circles when *Connected Longeing* (see p. 119), go back to an earlier exercise.

Photo F You can see that traveling to the right is difficult for Perle. It is common for horses being longed or worked on one line to experience more difficulty in this direction. They may be stiff on the right side as a result of only being handled from the left side.

contact, and allowing the spine to lengthen during movement. Most of all, it does not allow a horse to engage his hind legs and use his abdominal muscles. The horse may do what is being asked, but elasticity, resiliency, and soundness are often compromised or lost.

We have all seen horses react to flies landing on their body. Day after day they feel the same light touch of the fly. Why, then, do they so easily tune out human beings? I frequently hear the following: "My horse is not listening to me." "My horse is lazy." "My horse is stubborn." Horses tune out human beings or develop behavioral reactions when communication is not clear, or when they are handled in a way that throws them out of balance and disconnects them. The "elephant in the living room" is that we humans do not pay enough attention to how we use our own body when we work with horses. The compression in our body is transferred to our horse, and then we often blame the horse for not responding.

So why isn't everybody riding and handling horses in connection? Because we often fall into habitual, unconscious movement patterns—ineffective ways of using our body. Over time, compensatory patterns emerge, and inefficient movement creates more restricted, compressed movement in both horse and rider.

➨ Compression encompasses all those things that shut horses down, including retraction of the head and neck, and tightening or dropping the back to initiate movement. The result is shortened strides and loss of freedom of movement. Other byproducts of compression include overdevelopment of incorrect muscles; more concussion to the joints and skeleton; harder, more mechanical movement; and inactive hindquarters.

➨ Compensation—how a horse reacts to compression physically and emotionally—is not about bad behavior; it is a coping mechanism, a no-choice posture for the horse. It is like being stuck in a fight or flight situation in the body. Signs that a horse is compensating include lack of focus; a high head or a too curled neck; bracing anywhere in the body; stiffening during transitions or when changing di-

> ### Remember to Remember
>
> Connected Groundwork allows a horse to experience greater potential for freedom of movement and ease. As I see it, a horse is not being stubborn or disrespectful if he is not cooperating. Most likely, if he is unable to perform an exercise, he is experiencing an unfamiliar sensation, tightness, or discomfort somewhere in his body. If apparent tightness or discomfort persists after several sessions of Connected Groundwork exercises, the horse may require therapeutic support such as the Tellington Method, chiropractic, or massage.

rection; a raised head during transitions or when changing direction; suddenly changing tempo; backing up when starting an exercise; tripping; dragging the feet; spooking; fear of going through, over, or under things; exhibiting crabbiness; nipping or biting; and not wanting to be touched.

➨ Counterbalancing occurs in the Cycle of Disconnection when movement cannot flow freely through the horse because parts of the horse's body are compressed and "stuck." The rider works harder to try to create the desired movement and often becomes even more braced and unbalanced. The horse then adjusts by either bracing back harder or by mechanically counterbalancing the rider. This causes stress as parts of the horse's body are overtaxed from compensating for inefficient movement. Disconnection results in more labored work and/or evasions as horse and rider remain in a persistently disconnected pattern, and freedom of movement is lost.

First Step to Connection: Awareness

Get to know your own habitual patterns, such as pulling on the lead or reins, bracing with your back and shoul-

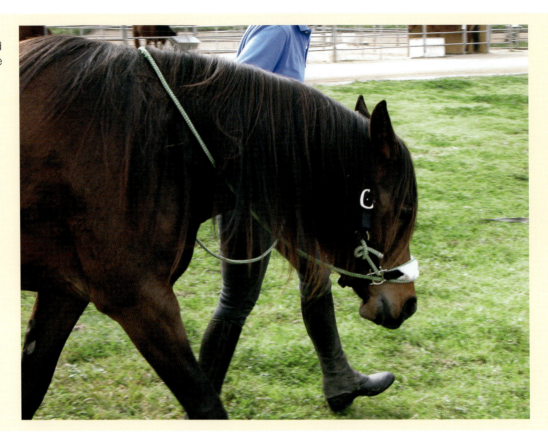

1.16 Thinking about it: This mare is walking and processing (see p. 7) the information presented during a Connected Groundwork session.

ders, and squeezing with your legs. All of these can lead to what I call a *negative equal-and-opposing cycle* (see p. 4). Fortunately, there are many ways in which you can turn a negative cycle into a positive one.

A *positive* equal-and-opposing action creates connection; a *negative* one creates compression. It is up to you to discern the difference and change the pattern. If the horse pulls on you and you pull back, you are caught in a negative equal-and-opposing cycle. But if he pulls and you *Comb the Line* (p. 51) and rotate (p. 54), you "diffuse the bomb" and invite him to reciprocate.

That's the magic of it; you don't get sucked into the vortex of his imbalance. You learn to be in charge of your own body, and when this happens, the horse learns to accept the connection and *Meet* you (p. 5).

As you can see, moving from patterns of disconnection to connection requires communication between horse and rider that travels from body to body and mind to mind, inviting reciprocity, observation, response, and

responsibility in both partners. For this transformation to occur, the following are necessary:

→ You must pay attention to your body.

→ Any time there is bracing in the horse or human, it needs to be *released*.

→ Every evasion needs to be observed as an out-of-balance situation with the horse usually on the forehand. The horse's body needs to recapture the freedom to move like a Slinky® without kinks, so he can constantly shift weight dynamically and work off his haunches rather than remain heavy on the forehand.

Most riders are willing to learn and are truly interested in doing what's best for their horse. One of the ways to achieve this is increasing rider/handler awareness. This includes the following:

→ι Having a clear picture of the desired result

→ι Knowing what is working

→ι Knowing what is not working and how to change it

→ι Being willing to change when something is not working

Many methods of teaching riding have become obsolete. The commands and words used by instructors—such as "squeeze," "push," and "pull"—create compression and mechanical movement in both horse and rider. At the same time, riders must also learn to change their own long-held habits and adopt new methods to shift themselves and their horses from:

→ι Bracing to releasing

→ι Holding to supporting

→ι Squeezing to alternating rhythmical movement

→ι Reacting to thinking

→ι Demanding to asking

→ι Repetitive drilling to "chunking" exercises into small segments and giving the horse time to process

If your horse is showing signs of disconnection and you stop or proceed to another exercise, it does not mean that you are "letting him get away with something" or that he has not learned anything. On the contrary, the horse will probably surprise you with the amount of information he has processed when you come back to the abandoned exercise 10 minutes later or the next day (fig. 1.16). Remember to be patient and observant. Above all, enjoy the process!

PART II

Exercises for the Handler

Become "Live Weight" to Help Your Horse Rebalance

Learning how to align, connect, and rebalance your own body lays the foundation for your success with Connected Groundwork and Connected Riding. This section of experiential exercises is designed to help you discover, sense, and resolve your predominant reaction when you are tense. You may habitually walk through life with a bit

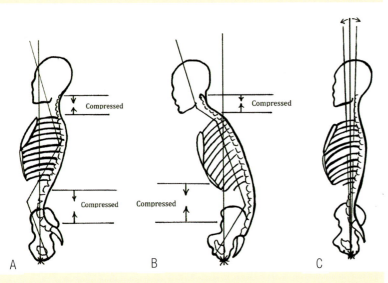

2.1 A–C An arched posture creates compression in the neck and lower back (A). A slumped posture creates compression in the front of the rib cage and back of the neck (B). *Neutral Posture/Pelvis* is the only position where the body automatically "buoys" (see p.7) and rebalances in motion (C).

of an arch or slump in your back and not realize that you can learn to be in "neutral" most of the time (figs. 2.1 A–C). Not only will this give you greater ease of movement and less stress, but it will make your work with horses more synchronized and congenial. While working with a horse on the ground or in the saddle, arching or slumping on your part initiates bracing. This makes your back, hands, and legs tighten to maintain uprightness, which prevents your core muscles from stabilizing your trunk and your entire body from working as a unit of integrated moving parts.

"Dead Weight" vs. "Live Weight"

Horses rely on stability and balance from our body to give them support and clear communication. When the handler/rider cannot balance in motion without bracing, the horse has no choice but to counterbalance and compensate by bracing in his own body. When the handler/rider braces or leans with any part of her body, it feels like a drag or "dead weight" (see p. 4) to the horse. This places considerable strain on the musculoskeletal system and can lead to lameness and other stress-induced injuries.

The single biggest gift you can give your horse is becoming "live weight," whether on the ground or in the saddle. A horse can feel the difference if you're braced against him or moving with him. When you learn to rebalance your body while remaining upright over your feet with your joints moving freely and without clamping on the horse, you can truly be "in sync" with his motion. "Live weight" is the state of natural dynamic alignment that allows the body to rebalance itself without bracing. As already discussed, I call this *Neutral Posture* or *Neutral Pelvis* (your "middle"). This is the process of *self-carriage* in humans.

When you are in *Neutral Posture*, both sides of your body—your arms, legs, and hips—work independently of each other, and the horse feels a *sequential, oscillating rhythm* coming from your body through the line or reins. This pulsating, alternating rhythm invites the horse to release tension and bracing patterns, as well as to participate and reciprocate. *Neutral Posture* is the *only* position in which the energy of your movement goes through to your horse's body, and the energy of his body comes back to you in an unbroken continuous circuit (see the Cycle of Connection on p. 11). It is the best way to build elasticity and lightness in your horse with the least amount of effort.

Why Neutral?

When you are not in *Neutral Posture*, movement becomes "stuck." The energy that originates in your feet does not go through to the pelvis and then to your hands; there is no *oscillating rhythm* pulsing through the line, reins, or hands. Instead, there is only a pulling sensation or a heaviness that engenders resistance from the horse (see Are You Leading a "Heavy" Horse, p. 109). When you are "draggy" like this, your horse will shut down or overreact in a negative equal-and-opposing cycle (see p. 16).

Being in *Neutral Posture* when handling or riding a horse allows you to meet resistance, such as a sudden spook or spin, with a "buoyant" response because your core muscles, such as the *psoas, obliques,* and *Rectus abdominus,* automatically engage to maintain your body's uprightness. If you are not in neutral and meet such resistance, you have to rely on the extremities—your arms and legs—to "grab" and "clamp" to find balance. Your core muscles will not automatically engage to rebalance you.

As you gain awareness and skill sitting, standing, walking, and riding in *Neutral Posture*, you will increasingly be able to override and diminish the horse's natural tendency toward fight or flight, which most often results from lack of physical or emotional balance. Practicing the postural exercises in this section brings you to a new awareness of how to move with less restriction and more balance. You will learn how to "float" over your hips and return to neutral when you fall out of balance. You will experience a grounded sensation because the core muscles of your torso automatically engage and give you stability. In neutral, your limbs and joints are free to move independently (both sides separately), adding strength and stability to your balance and a sense of support and connection to the horse. You will both enjoy the lightness, ease of movement, lack of tension, and security from working in connection that only comes from *Neutral Posture*.

What Is Neutral Posture?

Neutral Posture/Pelvis (your "middle") is not a fixed posture; rather, it is a dynamic place where you are ready at all times to move because your breathing and your expanding rib cage allows your body to "buoy" (see p. 7). Learning to distinguish the sensation of when your hips are tight and when they are released, and then being able to control it, affects how your horse feels you

Know Your Postural Habits

Are you aware of your postural habits? Have you ever noticed stress, fatigue, or exhaustion in your back, knees, or hip joints after standing, walking, or riding? Many of us unconsciously brace to counterbalance our body. Our static position, our stiffness, and our tightness are then transmitted to our horse. The first step toward learning to become "live weight" and dynamic in our posture is to become aware of our postural habits and patterns.

2.2 Poor posture such as I am demonstrating here leads to counterbalancing, stiffness, and bracing in both horse and handler/rider.

when you work with him from the ground or the saddle—whether you are braced or elastic.

Most people haven't been taught how to dynamically rebalance, and so as I've mentioned they fall into patterns of bracing and standing in a counterbalanced position, often locking one or both hips. The familiar "stand up straight and get your shoulders back" posture isn't the answer—it pushes the torso down and back, and compresses the pelvis, lower back, and hip joints. It is a fixed position that *inhibits* rather than *invites* freedom of movement.

When you're in *Neutral Posture*, your pelvis is neither tipped forward nor backward; your pelvis is aligned over the middle of the seat bones (*ischial tuberosity*) whether you are standing, sitting on a chair, or on your horse's back. In this ideal posture, your torso is neither arched nor slumped nor excessively wiggly

Building Awareness and Reeducating the Body through Movement

2.3 A–G Study this set of before-and-after photos. There are three "archers" and one "slumper," who—after learning to recognize their habitual postures—found neutral. Can you identify them? These examples show how people in everyday life forget to pay attention to how they use their body. (See more about arching and slumping on pp. 26 and 27.)

The exercises in this section will increase your awareness of your movement patterns. You will also practice nonhabitual movements to reeducate your body. Moshe Feldenkrais—an Israeli physicist and movement expert who created the Feldenkrais Method®—stated, "The nervous system can learn and change patterns through simple exercises of nonhabitual movement that do not cause fear or pain." This kind of movement creates new information in you, and in your horse's neural pathways. It allows you both to release old patterns of "holding" and habitual posture so you can feel and allow a broader, freer range of motion, as well as establish new, effective movement patterns. (For more about Feldenkrais work, see p. xv.)

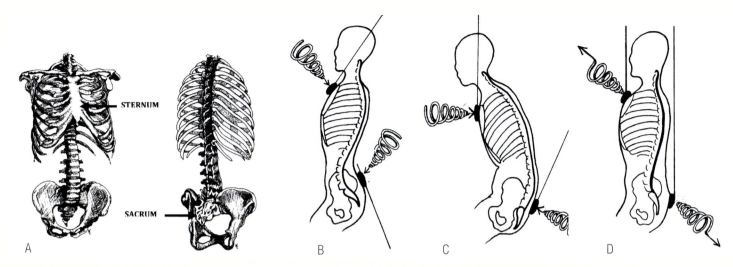

2.4 A–D Illustration A shows the position of the sternum and the sacrum—important reference points when finding neutral. When the body arches, as in B, it is very stiff and when in motion, creates bracing. The sternum and the sacrum are not parallel to each other. A slumped body, as shown in C, is really "dead weight," and it also creates bracing in motion. Again, the sternum and the sacrum are not parallel. Neutral, illustrated in D, is the only position where dynamic expansion can occur—the sternum and the sacrum are parallel, and there is room for the body to expand and lengthen—the sternum expands forward and up, and the sacrum expands backward and down.

(*hypermobile*). Your upper body stabilizes ("buoys") itself automatically, rebalancing with each stride, whether you're walking or riding, because the core muscles can engage without bracing. Each hip joint is free to move, allowing your legs and arms to move independently. When sitting or standing in neutral, the body is most stable, strong, and free so the limbs can be used effectively without restriction (figs. 2.4 A–D).

When your back is arched (hollowed) and your chest slightly lifted, your pelvis tips forward. In contrast, if your back is slumped and your chest slightly collapsed, the pelvis tips backward. When you are either arched or slumped—that is, *not* in *Neutral Posture*—your back, neck, shoulders, and joints begin to hold tension and may become stiff and painful. Over time, people who chronically fail to find *Neutral Posture* complain of back problems, joint pain, and body aches. When you feel stiff or painful anywhere on your body after riding, it is again because you probably are not riding in neutral.

The hypermobile individual, in contrast to the excessively stiff one, undulates back and forth across the vertical like a willow tree in the breeze, the equivalent of a "rubber-necked" horse that can never seem to move straight. There is excess movement through the lumbar vertebrae; the upper body does not work as a unit with independently moving hips, arms, and legs.

Learning to recognize, attain, and remain in *Neutral Posture* is critical to building a solid foundation with horses because it enables you to connect with your horse in a powerful, effective way.

Eight Exercises to Achieve Neutral Posture

The following exercises will help you achieve *Neutral Posture* and reduce tension in your body while you are working with your horse on the ground and under saddle. Every time you are in *Neutral Posture*, you can achieve more with less effort.

By methodically going through each of the following standing and sitting exercises, you will notice the contrast of how different positions affect your body's ability to make tiny movements—as small as an eighth or sixteenth of an inch—in front of and behind an imaginary vertical plumb line through your torso (see p. 7). You can experience the sensation best on a chair without a horse to control or your legs having to "think" at the same time. These exercises, therefore, isolate your body reactions without the complication of a horse triggering the very patterns you are working to overcome. (Note: You can also do them with your horse from the ground or mounted, taking contact on a piece of mane or pressing on the pommel of your saddle, just as you will press or take contact on the back of the chair.) These exercises enable you to imagine "lengthening" between your sternum and sacrum, which releases compression and engages your core muscles to stabilize your body, while achieving the sensation of lightness.

If you don't stop to learn these subtle sensations now, you won't notice the difference between having an elastic connection with your horse, and not. Your horse may be obedient but he will not *reciprocate*—that is, he will not take responsibility for his end of the partnership by maintaining the connection you initiate.

The key to *Neutral Posture* is not the *strength* of your core muscles per se, although you of course need a measure of strength to maintain your posture. Unless you know *from the inside out* how to identify ineffective posture and can learn to recognize the contrast, you will not know how to find it when you're beside the horse or in the saddle.

1   Finding Neutral Posture (Sitting)

The purpose of this exercise is to help you recognize the contrasts between being arched or slumped, and *Neutral Posture*. The trick to finding "neutral" is to experiment with the three postures. Make any changes in your posture slowly so that you can notice what is happening inside you.

→ Sit on the edge of a chair and experiment with a very tiny "buoying" movement—swaying your upper body back and forth across an imaginary vertical plumb line.

→ If you *raise* your sternum (your breastbone) slightly (arch), what happens to the tiny movement (fig. 2.5

A)? Does the buoying take more effort? Is the back-and-forth movement even or jerky?

→ If you *drop* your sternum slightly (slump), what happens to the movement (fig. 2.5 B)? How does this back-and-forth movement differ from the movement when you lift the sternum? Which posture allows you to move with the most ease?

→ Notice how it feels when the buoying movement is so subtle that it would hardly be visible if someone were watching (fig. 2.5 C). When you have found the place where the movement takes the least effort, seems the easiest to maintain, and is even, then chances are you have found your "middle" (*Neutral Posture/Pelvis*).

Now that you have a better idea where *Neutral Posture* is, experiment how being in neutral—or not—affects your breathing.

2   Breathing from Your "Middle"

Understanding the correlation of how your posture affects your breathing helps you override unconscious bracing patterns when you do groundwork or ride. Most people go through their day without making full use of their capacity to breathe. If you are slightly arched or slightly slumped in your posture, it is impossible to experience true expansion of the rib cage, effective use of the diaphragm, and a sensation of "floating" the upper body over the pelvis—as if your upper body is filled with helium or you are standing up to your neck in a pool of water. In other words, when you are not in *Neutral Posture*, your breathing is shallow.

There would be far less stress in people's bodies at the end of the day if they consciously paid attention to their breathing five or six times during a 12-hour period. And imagine the difference the horse feels in your body when you breathe from your "middle"! The following exercise helps you experience what it feels like to breathe more fully.

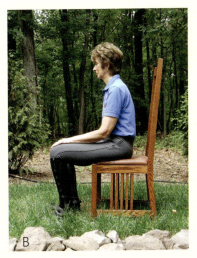

2.5 A–C Notice the subtle differences in my body in these three postures. (Note: Some women have more of an arch in their back than I do.) Arched (A), slumped (B), and in neutral (C) on the edge of a chair.

→| Sit on the edge of your chair and find your neutral as you did in the first exercise in this section (p. 24). Notice how you are breathing in and out.

→| Place your hands on your lower abdomen below the belly button (fig. 2.6 A). Take several breaths, allowing your belly to expand into your hands. Notice the contrast of the sensation in your hands as you change your body from neutral to arching or slumping. What differences do you observe? When is there less movement between your hands? When is there no expansion between your hands?

→| Make "soft" fists and place them on each side of your waist (fig. 2.6 B). Repeat the above steps. What is the sensation there?

→| Move your "soft" fists just below your armpits (fig. 2.6 C). Again breathe and become aware of how your body moves according to your position.

→| Next, turn and straddle the chair while taking contact on the sides of the chair's back. Observe the sensation of your rib cage expanding as you "breathe into your back."

→| Without tightening your hands or back, increase your contact with the chair, stretching back from your elbows and upper arms, and notice what happens (figs. 2.7 A–C). Are you able to maintain your "full" back and open rib cage while increasing contact?

→| As you take contact on the back of the chair, observe what happens to your rib cage and breathing when you slightly tip backward, going behind the vertical. How does the quality of contact change? What happens if you arch and "sit up" or slightly collapse the sternum (slump)? Does your back tighten or your breathing change? Does the contact get harder? Notice what you need to do to "release" from tense postures and feel the expansion in your rib cage and the sense of "breathing into your back and belly" once again.

This exercise simulates what often happens when we lead or ride horses—we unconsciously tighten our back or hands and hold our breath, especially when having to set a boundary, such as when asking for a halt or transition. This creates bracing patterns and resistance in the horse, who meets the tightening with an equal-and-opposing reaction (see p. 4). Here you learn

2.6 A–C Place your hands on your belly to feel movement under your hands as you breathe (A). Then place your hands on each side of your waist and notice your ribs expanding as you inhale (B). Finally, place "soft" fists below your armpits. When you are in neutral, you will notice expansion under your hands as you breathe. When you are arched or slumped, you will feel little or no movement.

2.7 A–C Taking contact on the back of the chair, in an arched position (A), a slumped position (B), and in neutral (C).

that as you increase contact on the sides of the back of the chair, you can feel your rib cage expanding and contracting as you breathe. You see that changing the degree of contact needn't require your hands or back to become tense.

→ Finally, experiment with the following while sitting or standing: Place one hand on your sternum, palm *against* your body. Place the other hand on your sacrum (the flat place on your lower back between your hips), palm *away* from your body. Notice the sensation of expansion and lengthening between your hands. Now leave one hand on the sternum and move the hand on your back to just above your waistline and again notice the sensation of expansion between your hands (figs. 2.8 A & B). Understanding the correlation of how your posture affects your breathing helps you override unconscious bracing patterns when do groundwork and ride.

3 Arching (Hollowing) vs. Neutral Posture

Now that you have established a contrast between arching, slumping, and *Neutral Posture* as it affects your breathing, the next step is learning how to find *Neutral Posture* by noticing how your back and rib cage interact.

→ Close your eyes and place your hands on your sternum and sacrum. Find *Neutral Posture* (fig. 2.9 A). Slowly lift your sternum and feel the change under your hands and in your lower back. Now slowly release and let the sternum return to where you started. Do this two or three times, very slowly, and notice the relationship between your sternum and sacrum.

→ Now repeat the above but with your back hand higher, placed just above your waist (fig. 2.9 B). Notice when the back hollows and when it feels flatter and

2.8 A & B With one hand on the sternum and the other on the sacrum, notice the sensation of expansion and lengthening between your hands (A). You will experience more movement when you move your hand from your sacrum to above your waist because your ribs have more ability to expand (B).

2.9 A–D First I find *Neutral Posture* with my eyes closed and my hands on my sternum and sacrum (A). With my eyes still closed, I slowly lift my sternum with my hands on my sternum and above my waist (B). When I arch (hollow) my back with my left hand on my sacrum, my left arm feels constrained (C). When I arch my back with my hand above my waist, it feels as if my front hand has more pressure on it than my back hand (D).

"fuller." If your postural habit is to arch or hollow your back when sitting on a horse or under stress (such as your horse tensing up), practice the sensation of "softening" in the lower back, allowing it to fill and flatten. This will help to override the habit of unconsciously hollowing and tensing.

→ Experiment with moving your thighs as if you are alternately moving your knees back toward your hips. The movement feels like peddling a unicycle backward. It involves engaging the thigh muscles, and when you are in *Neutral Posture*, this movement is very easy, and it feels as if the bones slide easily inside your skin. When you lift the sternum (arch), notice how this movement loses its ease and subtlety. Again, this shows how *Neutral Posture* is the only place where your arms and legs have independent movement from your torso.

4 Slumping (Collapsing) vs. Neutral Posture

→ Again, with your eyes closed, place your hands on your sternum and sacrum and find *Neutral Posture*. Slowly drop the sternum a tiny amount (less than an inch) and feel the change under your hand on your lower back as you "slump." Repeat two or three times very slowly and notice the relationship between the sternum and sacrum (fig. 2.10 A).

→ Now repeat with your back hand just above the waist, always slowly returning your sacrum to the place where you began (fig. 2.10 B). Notice that when you slump, your lower back is rounder, and when you slowly open the rib cage and increase the distance between your belly button and sternum, it flattens as it was when you began in *Neutral Posture*. If your habit is to drop the sternum in stress or unconscious posture, remember this sensation of slowly opening the rib cage and lengthening the space between the sternum and belly button.

→ Now repeat the experiment from earlier, moving your thighs as if you are alternately moving your knees back toward your hips. When you drop the sternum (slump), this movement becomes difficult, as it did when you arched (see p. 27).

5 Checking for Neutral Posture (Sitting)

PART ONE: PRESSING

→ Turn a chair around and straddle it. Make a fist with each hand and press against the back of the chair. When you are in *Neutral Posture*, pressing the back of the chair feels even and your body stays soft. (*Note:* This is the way your body needs to feel when you do Connected Groundwork exercises such as *Shoulder Press*—p. 77.) Your spine feels as if it lengthens and your back stays soft; there is no need for bracing. It feels like the press of your hands goes through to your seat bones; you feel as if you are sitting deeper and more solidly in the chair without adding any effort.

→ When you slightly lift your sternum (arch), notice how the press feels more like a push. The push sends your body backward unless you brace against it (fig. 2.11 A). The push of your hands does not go through to your seat, and you may feel some discomfort in your lower back.

→ When you slightly lower the sternum (slump), the press against the chair again becomes a push. Your upper body feels unstable because there is no connection going through from your hands to your seat bones (fig. 2.11 B).

→ Return to *Neutral Position* (fig. 2.11 C).

2.10 A & B When I slump (collapse) with my hand on my sacrum, it feels as if I am squeezing myself together (A). When I slump with my hand above my waist, the arm reaching around to my back feels constrained, and there is more pressure on the back hand than the front hand (B).

PART TWO: TAKING CONTACT

→ While straddling the chair, take contact on the back of the chair (grip lightly on each side) and stretch back from your elbows (see *owning your elbows,* p. 7). This should feel like you are taking contact on the chair without incurring a pulling sensation from your hands.

→ Now take contact on the chair in first an arched and then a slumped position. Notice if you feel you are pulled forward, braced, or pushed backward.

→ Return to *Neutral Posture*. The contact should feel stable and supportive. As you take contact the triceps muscle contracts at the back of your upper arm, and your entire forearm has an upward, light, lifting sensation as your elbow moves slightly backward. This becomes an elastic connection to the horse on a line or via the reins. When your body is not in neutral, your forearm has a downward, heavy, forward sensation that feels as though you are taking contact from your hand rather than the back of

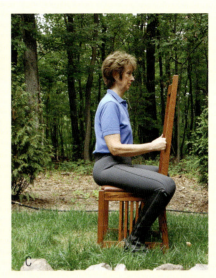

2.11 A–C I check my *Neutral Posture* by straddling a chair and pressing my fists against its back with an arch (A), slump (B), and in neutral (C).

your arm. This heavy sensation invites the horse to respond in kind.

While working your horse from the ground, you will notice an immediate difference in how the horse responds when you take contact in or out of neutral. When you are not in neutral and squeeze the line with your hand to take contact, the horse will feel a downward pulling and/or a heavy sensation, and you will feel as if you are pulling or being pulled on the line. When you use your hand to squeeze the line instead of gently stretching back from the elbow, the contact the horse feels is intermittent, stiff, and unclear.

PART THREE: ROTATION

In *Neutral Posture*, rotation refers to the intentional movement of your upper body (torso) turning over the hips. I use the term "rotation" to indicate turning on a level plane with the hips and shoulders parallel to each other, as opposed to tipping or twisting the torso, which drops the connection to the horse. Rotating in *Neutral Posture* allows natural independent movement in your

hips and limbs while maintaining stability in your upper body through engagement of your core muscles.

Torso rotation provides leverage, ballast, and support to the horse as you turn and change direction. It transmits a grounded and anchored sensation from your body to his. As a groundwork and riding aid, rotation helps to lighten transitions, prevent pulling (in horse or handler), and maintain an elastic connection on the line, lead, or rein.

It is critical to understand how to turn your torso so you do not tighten in your hips or lower back. When you offer rotation to your horse in a correct manner, he receives a stretching, gliding, directional shift, which helps him lighten and override habitual bracing patterns.

→ Straddle your chair and find *Neutral Posture* (check it by making soft fists and pressing against the back of the chair—see p. 28). Rotate your body to the *right*, and press on the *right side* of the chair back with the back of your *left fist*. Then rotate to the *left* and press on the *left side* of the back of the chair with the back of your *right fist*. When you are in neutral, pressing on the back of a chair feels even and your body stays

2.12 A–F I rotate to right and left in an arched position (A & B), a slumped position (C & D), and in *Neutral Posture* (E & F).

Checking Neutral Posture: The Shirt Test

2.13 The Shirt Test is an easy way to add a physical sensation to being in *Neutral Posture* as compared to arched or slumped.

Either standing or sitting, cross your arms in front of your body and grab your shirt on either side so that it feels like a snug band on your back. Move from neutral, to arched, to slumped—when you are in neutral, the band will feel the widest. Try rotating to the right and to the left, again varying your position between neutral, arched, slumped, and back to neutral.

soft. (*Note:* This is the way your body, especially your lower back, needs to feel when doing Connected Groundwork exercises like *Shoulder Press* and *Heart-Girth Press*—pp. 77 and 78*)*. You may experience the sensation of your upper body going forward and up as your lower back goes back and down. As you press, notice that your back and shoulders do not need to tighten to maintain your balance.

→ When you lift or drop your sternum (arch or slump), does the press feel more like a push and do you feel less stable (figs. 2.12 A–D)?

→ Return to *Neutral Posture* (figs. 2.12 E & F).

2.14 A–C I stand in an arched position (A), a slumped position (B), and in *Neutral Posture* (C). The difference between the arching and the neutral photos may seem imperceptible at first glance. This is because we are so accustomed to seeing the arched, "stand up straight" posture. What may be difficult to discern is the effort being put forth to maintain the arched posture, whereas in the neutral stance there is no effort needed.

2.15 A–C I check my Neutral Posture by pressing on the top of the back of a chair in an arched position (A), a slumped position (B), and in neutral (C).

6 Finding Neutral Posture (Standing)

→ After you have familiarized yourself with finding your "middle" in a chair, stand with your feet about shoulder-width apart. Remember the sensation of *Neutral Posture* when you were sitting, and notice if your tendency while standing is for your back to be slightly hollow, flat, or slightly rounded.

→ If you *raise* your sternum slightly (arch), what happens (fig. 2.14 A)?

→ If you *drop* your sternum slightly (slump), what happens (fig. 2.14 B)?

→ Return to *Neutral Posture* (fig. 2.14 C) and experiment with the sensation of moving your legs alternately (almost imperceptibly) as if your feet were ankle-deep in mud. Imagine the sensation you get when you pull off a boot. When you are in *Neutral Posture*, it feels as if the bones move easily inside your legs, and your thighs have a lot of lifting power. When you are arching or slumping, the movement takes more effort and is less subtle.

→ It is very important to remember to "unlock" your knees when standing. Close your eyes and lock your knees and then unlock them. What effect do the two different positions have on your upper body? Your lower back?

7 Checking for Neutral Posture (Standing)

→ Stand facing the back of a chair. You should be close enough to put your fingertips on the back of the chair without reaching.

→ Press lightly on the top of the back of the chair in an arched position (fig. 2.15 A). When you are arched, the press on the back of the chair feels like a push. There is stress on your upper body and lower back. Moving your legs minutely feels forced. The weight on your feet is on your heels and the press from your hands cannot be felt in your feet. Your position is not stable. The sensation is one of being pushed back and down.

→ Press on the top of the back of the chair in a slumped position (fig. 2.15 B). When you are slumped, the

2.16 A–C Raise your knee to help find the "crease" in the front of your hip joint (A). Notice how gently pressing in the crease slightly moves your torso like a buoy (B). Locking the knees not only tightens your lower back and upper body, it affects the muscles in front of the hip joint, thereby adding stress to the hip flexors and pelvic muscles (C).

press on the chair is again more of a push. There is stress on your upper body as well as through your hips and upper thighs. Small movement in your legs is awkward. The weight on your feet is in your heels and the press from your hands does not go into your feet. Your position is not stable. The sensation is heavy and pushing, and your upper body may tilt forward as your entire body is sent backward.

➫ When you are in neutral (fig. 2.15 C), the contact of your hands on the chair feels firm and soft. There isn't any stress in your body, and you can move your legs minutely with ease. The weight on your feet is evenly distributed, and you can feel the press from your hands in the soles of your feet. Your position feels stable. You may feel the sensation of your upper body "floating" up and forward as you press.

8   Opening the Hip ("Crease Release")

➫ Begin by finding the front of your hip joint: Place the heel of your hand on your hip bone with your fingers locating the crease between your torso and the top of your thigh. Lifting up your knee helps you find the fold between your leg and torso (fig. 2.16 A). Locate the point along this crease that is closer to the midline of your body (when you press inward

as your knee is slightly raised, you may notice a tiny indentation).

➫ Now stand in *Neutral Posture* and gently press into the indentation of the crease on both hip joints with your fingers (fig. 2.16 B).

➫ Next, stand with your knees locked with your fingertips in the crease (fig. 2.16 C). Do you notice how the crease is flatter? What happens to the little indentation? Does it disappear? Do your fingers feel "pushed out" of the crease? Does your torso "buoy"?

When the knees are locked the hip joint is braced and you are on the human "forehand." Notice what happens when you unlock your knees. Does the crease "release" to soften and allow the tiny indentation to reappear? Are your fingers nestled in the crease? The "buoy" of your torso should be free to move over your hips again.

When the front of the hip joint is "soft" and your knees are unlocked, there is a sensation of your upper body lightening and "floating forward" to initiate movement. Floating forward over your hips is a key sensation that conveys readiness for movement to the horse, both from the ground and under saddle.

Equipment & Connected Leading Basics

3.1 A–I When you unconsciously pull or hang on the horse's head and neck, you "train" the horse to brace when you take up contact. In contrast, *Connected Leading* helps the horse use his spine, stretch his topline, and move with you willingly, as if you are one being.

▌ Why We Lead in Connection

Connected Leading is the foundation for all Connected Groundwork exercises and the primary tool to reshape your horse's posture. If your horse has never been ridden, *Connected Leading* helps him carry weight (his and yours) more efficiently from the start. If he is already under saddle and using himself ineffectively, it aids in changing his posture to improve his way of going and overcome bracing habits (figs. 3.1 A–I). This section is really about learning to lead and halt your horse in a

different way—so he is better able to carry himself, use his spine, and stretch his topline.

By leading your horse in *Neutral Posture* (p. 20), you can override bracing and tension patterns in both you and your horse. If your horse has under-saddle issues, the place to begin undoing them is on the ground. Observe how you hold the lead rope, Connected Groundwork line (see p. 37), or reins. Take note if you tend to hop on your horse even when he is cold or tight.

I'm going to offer you new ways of leading and halting your horse from the ground that allow him to

"soften" each of his body parts, from head to tail, while integrating and differentiating them. Each body part is then able to do its own job under saddle. You are about to learn a new way of supporting your horse's head and body so he is better able to rebalance and move freely forward, which strengthens his pushing power and ability to carry weight, and improves his walk.

It is commonly known that the walk is the "most important" gait. This means that leading a horse (which is most often at the walk) has a critical influence on this gait under saddle. When you allow a poor quality walk from the ground, you will have the same poor quality walk under saddle. Whether you are leading your horse from his stall to his paddock, to the arena, or onto a trailer, you are *always* affecting the quality of his walk. Once your horse is able to carry himself, he will have a free walk with purpose on a loose line, and you can *Slide Up* (p. 49) and reestablish connection as a reminder when necessary.

Leading the Dance: First Steps

Have you ever danced with someone who really knew how to lead? Think about how secure you felt knowing where to step next. Remember the feeling of gliding across the floor? That is what the horse wants to feel from you—the sensation of connection and being in sync. The secret to this magical—and elusive—sensation begins with your body being in *Neutral Posture* so your joints can move freely and your limbs can be independent.

Why do I mention this again? Because rebalancing yourself "to neutral" on the ground or in the saddle is

a continuous dynamic process— it's not something you "get" and then move on. It takes *conscious practice* to become *unconsciously competent*. It requires *remembering to remember* to check in with your body, and to ask (and keep asking!): "Am I bracing somewhere? Am I breathing from my belly?" Being in *Neutral Posture* is now the foundation for all work you do with your horse.

Whether you're standing at the end of a lead line or working on *Connected Longeing* (p. 119), being in neutral, with a "crease" in the hip joint (see p. 32), "soft" lower back, unlocked knees, and your arms free to move are all essential. This means your body is free to access your core muscles, your torso can rotate easily, the contact from your elbows will feel elastic to the horse, and your connection will feel inviting instead of braced or tense.

Note: Whenever things start to fall out of balance with the horse—whether in these early exercises on the ground or later in your schooling under saddle—immediately check in with yourself (see p. 20). Only when you are in tune with your own body can you be in sync with your horse. (You will also learn to monitor your horse before and after each exercise to assess his progress—see p. 43.)

Equipment

You can do Connected Groundwork with standard equipment you probably already own. I explain its use in this section. Over time you may find that you desire a closer level of communication with your horse. I have refined

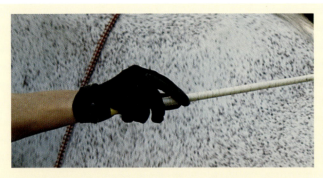

3.3 Sturdy gloves are a good safety precaution when doing Connected Groundwork.

the design of an alternative halter and stretchy ground-work "lines" that facilitate such communication. I describe their benefits and use beginning on p. 37.

Leather Gloves

I strongly recommend that you wear *form-fitting leather gloves* for all types of groundwork (fig. 3.3). Should a horse startle while doing groundwork exercises, gloves allow you to respond quickly by allowing the line or reins to slip through your fingers without fear of "rope burn" or injury. Although students and clinic attendees have on occasion mentioned that they "feel" less with gloves on, I've noticed that they seem to be lighter with their contact and smoother with their movements on the line.

Standard Halter and Lead Rope

You only need a snug-fitting, standard leather or nylon halter, and a chain lead (or soft lead—see p. 39) to get started with Connected Groundwork exercises. However, as I have mentioned, you may desire the better feel the specialized equipment I've developed can give you.

If you are using a conventional halter, choose one you can adjust to fit as snugly as possible around the horse's nose and face so it is not sliding all over the place. The throatlatch should be snug enough so the halter maintains lateral stability without choking the horse. Adjust the side cheekpieces so the noseband comes just below the cheekbones. (If the halter still slides around—and when you begin groundwork in motion and *Connected Longeing* (pp. 102 and 119)—I strongly suggest transitioning to the Connected Groundwork halter.)

Be sure you can run a line (see p. 37), or chain or soft lead rope, through the square rings on the side of the halter. Many lead ropes have large snaps that won't fit through the side rings. Whatever you use for a groundwork line should be light and flexible, with a bit of a "nubby" feeling as your hand slides up and down it. I ask people not to use a smooth or too-thin line—such as is common in climbing ropes—because if the horse is heavy or a challenge in any way, the tendency to grip these ropes {brace} is far greater. I recommend a line that is cotton or nylon and loosely woven. It shouldn't be too thick so it can be threaded through the halter.

3.4 A–C A too-loose regular halter slides around on the horse's face, dulls communication between handler and horse, and creates a drag on the horse's head (A). A regular halter that fits the horse well and is adjusted properly allows you to fully realize connection on one line (B).

Connected Groundwork Halter

For many years, I did groundwork in my clinics with the horses wearing a regular halter. I became increasingly frustrated because a standard halter tended to slide around on the horse's face as I tried to execute minute and specific movements in the poll. Even when I "snugged up" the halter by threading the line through it to help take up the slack, it was still too loose and bulky.

With the aid of my colleague Nancy Camp (she's also the artist responsible for the illustrations in this book), I developed a prototype Connected Groundwork halter. This halter cradled the horse's head and fit snugly. It allowed me to move the horse's head slightly to influence the poll without "wagging" the horse's head or having the halter slip around into his eye. I continued refining the design to be more precise to fit the many shapes and sizes of horses—we now offer small, medium, and large-sized Connected Groundwork halters on our Web site (www.connectedriding.com).

Benefits of the Connected Groundwork Halter

The Connected Groundwork halter is adjustable in three places so it can fit different head shapes. The halter does not slip or twist across the face, and it has a fleece lining, which is gentle on the horse's nose (fig. 3.5). Instead of a ring on the noseband under the horse's chin, there are "squares" on each side. By running the line through the side squares, the horse receives a clearer message than he would with the line attached under his chin.

It should be noted that this halter is not intended for tying or for purposes other than Connected Groundwork. It does have a breakaway leather poll piece.

The goal of Connected Groundwork is to communicate clear, quiet, and specific differentiation of movement to the horse. When you do this work in a loose halter, it actually *disconnects* you from the horse. It creates bracing in his head and neck because the horse feels a jerky and harsh movement from the halter. What I appreciate about the Connected Groundwork halter is the way it allows the person leading to convey a subtle message to the horse without our usual habits of "doing"—pushing, pulling, or yanking.

3.5 A properly adjusted Connected Groundwork halter fits snugly and allows the handler to communicate clear, quiet, and subtle movements to the horse. Here you see the line attached on both sides (see p. 38).

Of course, even with the Connected Groundwork halter, these things may still occur. It is up to each of us to bring our own awareness and sensitivity to the horse, regardless of equipment and circumstance. The halter is only as useful as our ability to lead with it from our Neutral Posture.

Connected Groundwork Line

Originally, I began my groundwork exercises using the Tellington Method's soft Zephyr lead instead of a standard lead rope with a heavy snap (see p. 39). As the Connected Groundwork system developed, a different type of lead line became necessary—one that was easy to loop and grasp in one hand and not too slippery, with the ability to "give" and stretch a tiny bit, and thread easily through the halter from both sides. It also had to be long enough to do the first phase of *Connected Longeing* (p. 119).

The Connected Groundwork line is made of woven marine nylon that has a "nubby" feel and a small amount of give. It is 21 feet long (although for smaller horses, 18 feet is adequate. If you are working with a long line on a smaller horse, you can shorten the line by tying a knot near the horse's withers.)

A single line is used for all of the initial standing, walking, and *Connected Longeing* groundwork. A second line is used for advanced *Two-Line Longeing* with a surcingle, which I do not cover in this book.

How to Fit the Connected Groundwork Halter and Line

Here you see how to thread the line through the halter on one (figs. A–I) or both (figs. A–L) sides. Fitting the groundwork line from both sides of the halter enables you to switch sides easily without stopping to reconfigure your equipment.

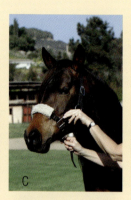

3.5 A–L Adjust the crownpiece so the noseband is below the base of the cheekbone (A). Depending on the horse's head shape, the noseband may be very close to the cheekbone. The cheekpiece should fit snugly to keep the halter from sliding from side to side (B). Adjust the buckle on the noseband so it is snug, allowing you to move the head with great precision (C). A well-adjusted Connected Groundwork halter still has room for you to slip your fingers beneath the noseband and cheekpiece (D). Insert the line through the nearside square, from the outside, in and down (E). Bring the line over the top of the noseband in preparation for threading it back through the offside square (F). Thread the tip of the line down and under the noseband, bringing it from the inside to the outside of the offside square (G). Pull it through so that you have enough line to go up to the ring above the cheekpiece amd tie a slipknot (H). Slip the end of the line from the inside to the outside of the top ring and pull a small amount of line through the ring, securing the line with a slipknot (I & J). Take the free end of the line and repeat these steps from the opposite side of the halter, forming an "X" over the horse's nose (K). Be sure that the crossover point is centered on the noseband. Now you can work from both sides of the horse, as needed. A correctly fitted Connected Groundwork halter and line enable you to maintain a snug contact without pulling on the horse's head (L).

Tellington Method® Chain Lead and Zephyr Lead

Linda Tellington-Jones' Tellington Method uses a 6-foot lead with a 30-inch chain attached at one end for some exercises (fig. 3.6 A). Although chains are sometimes controversial, I find them a useful tool to give a clear, light message to a very large horse, a stallion, or a horse that has not yet learned how to find his balance while

> ### Remember to Remember
>
> Because the Connected Groundwork halter must be snug to function properly, loosen and readjust your halter each time you use it by opening and refastening the buckle under the noseband.

being led. This can also be considered a safety measure, particularly when a smallish person is leading a tall or massive horse. The purpose of the chain is to support the horse so he can rebalance himself while being led. *It is not to be used as a means of punishment or co-*ercion. The Tellington Method's chain lead has a nylon line attached to the chain that is easy to comb, slide, and lengthen through your fingers

The soft Zephyr lead is a 6-foot flat lead with a sturdy (but soft) 30-inch climbing rope and lightweight snap attached at one end (fig. 3.6 B). The soft end of the line makes this a useful lead to use with young or extremely sensitive horses.

Tellington Wand

It was 1986 when I was first introduced to my mentor Linda Tellington-Jones and her Tellington Method. She used an instrument she called "the wand"—a 4-foot (or longer) white dressage whip (fig. 3.7). But the change in name denoted a change in meaning and purpose. Linda explained that the wand is used as an extension of your arm. I now use the wand as an aid to touch and stroke horses in the places that may be "stuck" (see p. 9) and to give them rhythm, encouragement, and soothing, as needed. The reason I recommend the Tellington Wand in particular is because it is a made of rigid fiberglass, so it is light, yet it feels firm and soothing to the horse. Standard dressage whips tend to be flexible and therefore "stingy" to the horse's skin. Again, the purpose of the wand is to support, *not to punish,* the horse. It is to bring awareness to his body and to his movement.

Tellington Wands come in various sizes: 36, 40, 44, and 48 inches in length. Most of the time I work with the longest length, but if you are of small stature, or your horse is small, you can choose one of shorter length.

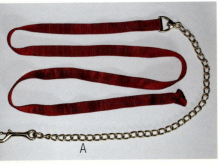
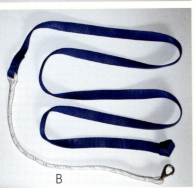

3.6 A & B The Tellington Method's chain lead is 6 feet long with a 30-inch chain at one end (A). It is easy to comb, slide, and lengthen through the fingers. The soft Zephyr lead offers a lighter connection than a standard lead rope and enables you to thread the line easily through a regular halter (B).

3.7 The Tellington Wand is a long, white, rigid dressage whip made of fiberglass.

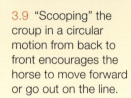

3.8 A–D "Stroking" the back with the wand calms the horse, brings body awareness, and helps the horse feel his back (A).Stroking the chest at the standstill helps the horse lower his head, slow down, and "soften" the base of his neck, and doing so while walking can modulate his pace and encourage the horse to "telescope" his neck (B & C). Stroking the front legs with the wand reduces tension and helps horses become aware of their feet (D).

3.9 "Scooping" the croup in a circular motion from back to front encourages the horse to move forward or go out on the line.

If you would like to try Connected Groundwork and do not have a wand, take a walk in the woods and pick a sturdy, straight branch at least 2½ feet long, or use a bamboo stick (not a dowel), which you can buy at your local garden center.

Uses of the Wand

This stiff, light piece of equipment is to be used as a "rhythm-giver" or a "pointer" to identify a body part that needs to yield or soften. A wand also helps create boundaries and can encourage the horse to increase energy and movement, or to slow down and stop.

Sometimes people are concerned that their horse "doesn't like" or is afraid of the wand. I believe this is due to tension in the horse's body, or the horse was hurt or frightened in some way by a whip at some point in the past. Your horse will learn to rely on the wand like a musician with a conductor's baton. *Stroking*, *flicking*, *scooping*, and *tapping* motions, as well as using the wand as a *boundary*, provide clear supportive signals.

→ **Stroking:** "Stroking" the horse's body with the wand can soothe, bring awareness, and delineate areas that are tight and braced (figs. 3.8 A–D). Stroking is also used to encourage the horse to soften the base of his neck and "telescope" his neck into contact. Stroking the wand on the horse's chest slows his rhythm and aids in the halt.

→ **Flicking:** There is a feathery end on the tip end of the wand (see fig. 3.7, p. 39). This is useful for lightly and

Work from Both Sides of Your Horse

Although most of the exercises in this book are shown from the left side of the horse for consistency, be sure to practice them from both sides. The exercises are presented in a logical learning sequence for both you and your horse, but you can initiate any exercise from either side and do them in any order.

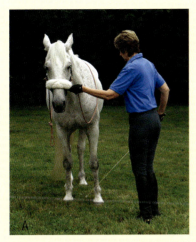

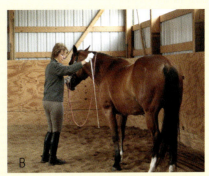

3.10 A–C "Tapping" the lower leg can be a signal for the horse to back up (A). Tapping the shoulder helps the horse yield and shift his weight to rebalance (B), and tapping across his barrel encourages his ribs to yield and his hind legs to keep moving (C).

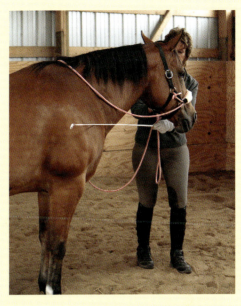

3.11 I am using the wand as a boundary by bringing it to the horse's opposite shoulder.

gently tickling the horse in more sensitive areas, such as his nose or mouth, to ask him to pay attention or move away from your space. "Flicking" is a quicker tickling motion used to give the horse direction or encouragement to move. This is usually done toward the neck, shoulder, or belly area, depending upon the exercise. (See more on this on p. 126.)

→❙ Scooping: "Scooping" with the wand is a circular motion to signify directional movement. This can be used on the croup to signal forward movement, or in *Connected Longeing,* as a cue to send the horse out on the line (fig. 3.9).

→❙ Tapping: "Tapping" is another way to bring awareness to segments of the horse's body that may be "stuck" and bracing (figs. 3.10 A–C). You can gently yet firmly tap along the neck or the inside shoulder when you want the horse to yield or soften. I sometimes use the knob on the end of the wand to tap a horse near the poll or along the neck from the sad-

dle when walking or trotting to say, "Hey there, you can release this part, too." I often use tapping on the horse's body—at the shoulder and right behind the heart-girth area, as a "rhythm-giver" when riding. I think of the wand as a paintbrush that helps me sculpt the horse's posture.

→❙ Using as a boundary: When training in the Tellington Method, I learned to use the wand as a "boundary" (fig. 3.11). I use it in this way in many of the Connected Groundwork exercises. Bringing the wand to the opposite shoulder helps a horse balance in a halt.

Tellington Wands are extremely useful as a schooling aid, both in groundwork and ridden work. For additional information, I recommend Linda Tellington-Jones' books on her training methods (see *Recommended Reading,* p. 137).

Holding the Wand and Line in the Same Hand

It is best to hold the wand and line in the same hand so you can tap the horse as you walk along with him. Here's how:

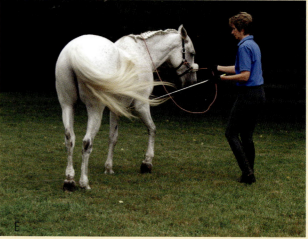

3.12 A–E When working on the left side of the horse, hold the wand in front of your body with the knob end between the your left pinky and the base of your left hand (A). Add the line, running down between your left forefinger and thumb and exiting between your middle and ring fingers (B). To tap the horse's shoulder, point the wand across your body and back under your right arm (C). When working on the right side of the horse, reverse the scenario (D). When tapping the barrel, hold the wand in one hand and the line in the other (E).

▌Preparing the Horse to Walk Forward in Connection

Just as human dance partners find their first position when beginning a dance, so we must do with our equine partners. "Snugging up" to the halter and gradually moving out on the line is the first in a sequence of steps to connect with the horse, free up his movement, and sync your movements together.

When you start teaching your horse Connected Groundwork exercises at the walk, begin with the hand closest to the horse "snugged up" to the halter (when on the left side, your right hand, and vice versa—fig. 3.13 A). Horses that have been pulled on learn to re-

3.13 A & B When you begin Connected Groundwork exercises at the walk, start with the hand closest to the horse (on the left side, your right hand, and vice versa) "snugged up" to the halter (A). As the horse starts to carry himself, he will walk with you even when there is some slack in the line (B).

tract their head and neck and lock their poll to protect themselves. "Snugging up" to the halter lets you sense whether the horse is bracing (providing you are in (*Neutral Posture*—see p. 20).

As your horse progresses through the groundwork exercises, he will gradually begin to carry himself and walk with you, even when there is some slack in the line between your hand and the halter (fig. 3.13 B). If the horse shows signs of disconnection—lack of focus, rushing, or lack of forward motion—slide back up on the line and "snug up" on the halter, *Walk an "S"* (p. 102), *Slide Up/Slide Out* (p. 49) and reconnect with the horse to facilitate his rebalancing.

You will move from this first position to the following exercises: *Tracing the Arc* (p. 72), *Elephant's Trunk* (p. 74), *Slide Up/Slide Out* (p. 49), and *Walking S One Hand* (p. 102). *Tracing the Arc* ensures freedom in the head and neck as the horse bends through a curve. *Elephant's Trunk* also frees the base of the neck and ensures that changes of direction can be made with ease.

Losing (Dropping) Connection

When either you or the horse "loses connection," the contact will feel awkward, absent, or "heavy" because you are out of sync and rhythm with the horse. It is important to be aware of the sensation in your body when you have a connection to the horse and when you do not. Notice when you feel off balance when leading the horse. How do you react when you disconnect? Are you tense? Do you tend to try to "muscle" the horse? Become aware of your body then return to *Neutral Posture* and reconnect with the horse.

Slide Up/Slide Out supports the horse to take a connection on the line while maintaining forward motion. *Walking S One Hand* helps the horse stretch the muscles of his topline.

1 Assessing the Walk: A Baseline Exercise

PURPOSE

Assessing the Walk is key to becoming aware of the changes in your horse's movement patterns. By initially assessing his walk, you have a baseline observation by which to compare changes in his posture and stride. This exercise also begins developing your eye to observe equine movement patterns on the ground and under saddle.

PROCEDURE

→ Begin at the halt and observe your horse's posture.

Is his head higher than his withers?

Is he standing squarely or are his hind legs camped out behind?

Notice the definition of his muscles of the neck and across the topline. Are they smooth, bulging, or sunken?

▌Case Study: Party

with Connected Riding Founder Peggy Cummings

Be sure to observe and notice the differences in your horse before and after Connected Groundwork. (Note: I provide a number of Case Studies later in the book to further illustrate this point.)

"Party" is a 25-year-old Thoroughbred who was with me from 1990 to 1993 as a 7- to 10-year-old. Although he was winning "Mini-Prix" competitions, his owner was told he would never be sound if he continued in the way he was being trained. When he came to me, he bolted, was unsafe to lead, had been ridden in draw reins, and had been longed in side reins steadily for at least three years.

Party taught me about tight shoulders, which shortened his stride and made him unpredictable. When tense, his head would fly up, and he would bolt or buck and get very "prancey" when ridden. He also taught me about the damaging effects of compressive "gadgets" on a horse's body—his back was dropped behind the withers and he had tendon and hock problems. It was incredibly difficult to pick up his hind feet.

I did Connected Groundwork exercises with Party for about a month, with fantastic results. Party is proof that with consistent work by a kind and conscientious owner, an unhappy, unsound, and "dangerous" horse can become a functional, safe, loveable partner.

Before

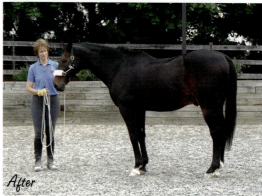

After

3.14 A & B Party before Connected Groundwork at age 25: Age-related stiffness, a dropped back, and tendon and hock problems are apparent (some of it is age). Party after Connected Groundwork: He stands comfortably in "neutral," his back has come up a couple of inches, he is calm and reliable, and he is a wonderful companion. Party was (and is) a very regal horse!

Does he continuously rest one hind leg or alternate resting both hind legs?

Does he ever stand squarely without being asked?

→▮ Walk your horse (or have another person walk him, so you can observe) from the left side on a loose lead in a straight line away from a wall or fence for about 10 meters (approximately 30 feet). Then, *turn to the right* and come back (fig. 3.15 A). As you do this, notice the quality of the walk. Notice how he initiates the walk and how he stops walking. Pay attention to how he makes the turn. Now walk

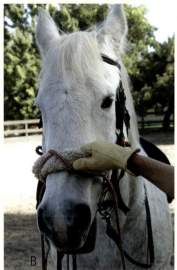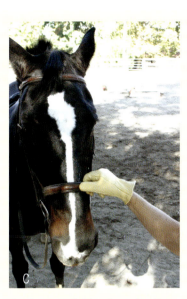

3.15 A–C Noticing how your horse walks before and after each Connected Groundwork exercise is essential to observing the resulting changes in his posture and stride. Begin by leading your horse on a straight line, first turning right and then left, and observe his movement (A). Next, hook the index and middle fingers of your right hand onto the noseband of the halter just off-center and lead your horse from this position, making note of differences in his movement (B). If you don't have a well-fitting halter, use the noseband on your bridle for this part of the exercise (C).

out a second time, this time *turning to the left,* and observe how he turns in this direction. Assess the following on both sides:

Does the horse raise his head and retract his neck, or does he release his head and neck as he begins walking, and as he stops?

Does the horse maintain his own space, or does he crowd or try to "walk through" you? Does he crowd on one side more than on the other?

Is the horse "light" or "heavy" (see p. 5) in the hand as he starts and stops walking?

Does he keep his walking rhythm through the turn, or does he slow down or lift his head?

Do his hind legs "push" or do they just "follow"— that is, do they have energy?

Is the horse dragging his front or hind feet?

Do the front feet seem to have a firmer footfall?

Does one front foot land heavier than the other front foot?

Does one hind foot land heavier than the other?

Is the horse eager to walk with you or does he walk ahead or lag behind?

Are the horse's hind feet stepping up into (or beyond) the prints of the forefeet?

Is he focused and tuned in, or distracted and shut down?

→ Standing on the left side of the horse, hook the index and middle fingers of your right hand onto the noseband of the halter, just off the center. If you

Exploring Connection on a Line

In Connected Groundwork, we begin by establishing connection on the line. Understanding the variables of establishing and maintaining connection on a line enables you to understand the relevance of connection with your horse in other work you do together.

What is "connection on a line"?

Connection on a line is an elastic, reciprocal, dynamic contact between horse and handler during groundwork (or through the reins while mounted). You are seeking the transference of energy from the horse's hind legs "coming through" his body into your hand or hands on the line.

What does connection on a line look like?

Connection on a line appears unbroken between the handler's hand(s) and the horse's head. It appears as if the two beings are moving together with freedom, ease, and lightness. There is a two-way communication going back and forth through the line. Neither horse nor handler appears to pull the other.

What does connection on a line feel like?

Connection on a line feels like a firm handshake. There is a "stretchy" elastic response when you *Meet and Melt* (see p. 5) with your horse. You get a sense of lightness and reciprocity— as if there is someone on the other end carrying on a conversation with you through feel.

How do you know you have it?

You know you have connection on the line when you can slide your hand from its position near the horse's head out toward the end of the line and feel reciprocal contact from the horse. As you walk or turn (remaining at least 2 feet away from the horse), he maintains this contact with you as well as energy and rhythm from his hind legs. It feels like you and the horse are moving together as a single unit.

What kind of feedback from your body tells you that you have connection?

You will experience a sensation of pulsating rhythm that goes from your hand(s) on the line all the way through to your feet— and yet you feel solidity on the ground. When you "take a connection" by stretching back with your elbow, you may notice a sensation in the core muscles of your torso as they engage in *Neutral Posture* (see p. 20).

What kind of feedback from your horse tells you that you have connection?

With some horses, connection may initially feel "heavy" until they loosen their body, begin pushing from their hindquarters, and lift their back. When this happens, you will notice the contact lightens considerably, even though it will still be "firm." Some horses start off with intermittent, very light contact, giving the sensation of a weak handshake (remember, you want a "firm" one), and eventually the contact gains in consistency. In both cases, you will sense the horse is responding when you *Slide Out* on a line (see p. 49) with an, "Okay, I will give you back contact," even though at first it may only last for two or three strides.

Is it difficult to establish connection on the line with some horses?

Some horses respond to your initial attempts at connection by raising their head and avoiding contact. In such cases, it is critical that you remain light in your hands, think "up" through your wrists (see p. 9), and stay "soft" in your back, as these horses do not yet trust contact. You may have to emphasize exercises at a standstill (p. 57) before moving on to groundwork in motion (p. 101). Other horses are "heavy" because they are stiff or carry undue tension in their head and neck and have bracing patterns in their body.

How do you handle a horse that tosses his head during Connected Groundwork exercises?

First check and see if you are being heavy with your hands or abrupt on the line. Are you in *Neutral Posture* and "soft" in your back as you work with the horse? It is important to begin Connected Groundwork exercises at a standstill, allowing the horse to get used to releasing his body while feeling your contact and connection. Then, the exercises *Walking "S" One Hand* (p. 102) and *Topline Stretch* (p. 107) can help the horse release tension while walking. It takes time for many horses to trust you enough to lower their head to balance, especially in movement.

Some horses that head-toss or are afraid of contact hold tension in the poll, head, or neck; are out of alignment in the atlas joint; have dental or jaw problems; or may have been "pulled on" during previous training and are now (understandably) head-shy. Be sure the horse is in good dental health and that his spine and joints are in proper alignment by consulting with a veterinarian, chiropractor, or other equine health professional.

What if a horse has an extreme bracing pattern?

Extreme bracing patterns are often the result of a horse being held together in a "false frame" (p. 4) or ridden with "gadgets" that invite the horse to brace against the aid for support. These horses have little sense of their own balance and become very tight and constricted in their movements. Connected Groundwork exercises are useful in reeducating the horse's musculature and nervous system to release habitual bracing patterns and replace them with the natural ability to move and rebalance.

How do I establish connection on a line?

Throughout this book I walk you through several ways you can begin to establish connection on the line. The first is through the *Slide Up/Slide Out* walking exercise (p. 49). The horse begins to connect on the line as he offers a reciprocal contact and maintains his forward motion. A second way, done at a standstill or walking, is to *Slide Up* the line to the halter, *Draw the Bow* (p. 49), and then slide back out on the line. A third way is to *Slide Up/Slide Out* and then *Comb the Line* (p. 51). This also can be done standing still or walking. A fourth way is to *Slide Up, Draw the Bow,* and then *Comb the Line* out about 2 feet, ending with the line in your left hand. Then place your right hand on the horse's neck and do *Caterpillar* (p. 64). Alternate going up the neck in *Caterpillar* with *Combing the Line*.

don't have a halter that fits well (see p. 36), use the noseband on your bridle for this exercise (figs. 3.15 B & C).

Keep your arm and wrist light as you lead the horse forward in this position. Walk your horse as you did in the previous step (in a straight line, then turning right and then left), and notice if the quality of the walk is different. Next, with your hand still hooked on the halter, walk a circle *to the right* about 6 meters (about 20 feet) in diameter. Notice if the quality of the walk is different than on the straight line. Circle again. As you continue walking this circle, observe the following:

Does the horse lower his head and neck?

Was the transition to the stop any different than when the horse was on a loose lead?

Does his posture look any different than before?

Has the horse taken any deep breaths, or licked and chewed?

Is his respiration any different?

→| With your hand on the halter as described in the previous step, walk a 6-meter circle to the left, keeping your arm light. Is the quality of the walk different? Is it slower or faster? Does the quality of the walk improve or deteriorate?

→| Next, lead the horse from the *right* side, and repeat the sequence with your left hand on the halter: walk a straight line, turn right and then left, walk 6-meter circles to the left and then to the right. What are the differences? How does one side differ from the other in quality and ease of gait, and willingness of the horse?

OBSERVATIONS

Most horses are not symmetrical. By *Assessing the Walk*, you see how different a horse can be from one

Leading a Human "Horse"—An Experiential Exercise

One way to really experience what it feels like to be a horse on the end of the lead line is to be led like one. Being led in connection and disconnection is a great way to sense and feel in your body why a handler in *Neutral Posture* is so essential to a horse. Here's an exercise to try with your riding buddies:

→ Take a line and make a snug figure eight around your partner's wrists (figs. 3.16 A–D). Tying the wrists in this fashion offers the clearest feedback to the "horse" and simulates being led in a Connected Groundwork halter.

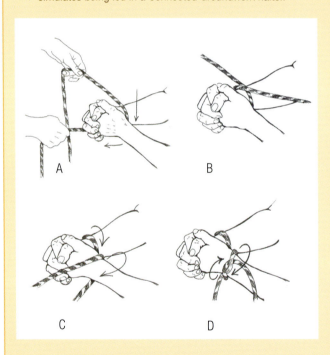

3.16 A–D The "horse" clasps her hands and the handler loops the line through the middle (A). Complete the loop around the "horse's" right arm, just behind the wrist bone (B). Bring the crossed line back through the middle and loop the line around the "horse's" left wrist to complete the figure eight (C). Tie a knot on the outside of the left wrist, and your "horse" is ready to go!

→ It's helpful for the "horse" to have her eyes closed to experience more clearly how you (the handler) are affecting her balance. Begin on the left side by leading the "horse" straight ahead on a loose line, making a couple of gentle turns in both directions (figs. 3.17 A & B). Try this in *Neutral Posture*, and then in an arched or slumped position (see p. 23). Stop. Share differences you both noticed.

→ Next, with the handler in *Neutral Posture*, *Draw the Bow* (p. 49), *Step to the Offside* (p. 52), and walk off so your "horse" feels what is like to be led with close contact in connection. Then *Walk an "S"* (p. 102), *Slide Out* (p. 49), *Comb the Line* (p. 51), and change direction. Discuss what you both experienced in this exercise.

Here are more leading experiments to further explore. Walk straight lines and gentle turns with:

→ the figure eight around the "horse's" wrists not snug (simulating a "loose halter").

→ the line tied *under* the wrists (what it is like when you attach a lead under the horse's chin instead of on the side).

→ the handler's wrist bent, instead of straight from elbow to "horse."

→ just ¼-inch of slack near the wrists.

→ the "horse" stiffening her body (what happens to the handler?)

→ a cue for a halt transition via *rotation* (see p. 54).

→ uneven ground or stairs, both in and out of connection. What happens?

3.17 A & B Here I give co-author Bobbie Jo Lieberman a taste of what it is like to be a horse led in connection.

This exercise has proven to be one of the most enlightening learning experiences for my students and clinic participants. It really helps you understand how much you can positively support the horse (or negatively impact him) through your body's posture and movement.

side to the other. Notice which change of direction is easier for the horse. I have found that horses are usually most free-moving when the handler is on the left side at the halter, walking in a circle to the right. When the handler is on the right side and circling left, it is more difficult for the horse. After Connected Groundwork exercises, walking in either direction and changing direction becomes easier because Connected Groundwork promotes the horse becoming more even and symmetrical, in both directions and on both sides of his body.

▌Walking in Connection: A Sequence of Foundational Exercises

The following building blocks of *Connected Leading* give you the tools to be successful. Practice each individually until they become second nature to you. Most of the exercises later in this book incorporate these first small but critical movements. The object of these exercises is to "soften" the joints, override bracing, and create a more *Neutral Posture* in the horse.

2 Slide Up/Slide Out and Draw the Bow

PURPOSE

Slide Up/Slide Out sends a rhythm from the line to the horse's poll to promote his natural oscillation (see p. 6). Minute oscillation of the poll encourages the horse to lower his head and neck and soften into contact. This is a foundational exercise that supports the horse, encouraging him to override bracing patterns and take connection on the line. It also helps him shift his weight in movement.

Draw the Bow creates an equal-and-opposing stretch—in two directions—between the handler's hands (see p. 4). *Draw the Bow* transmits the movement of the handler's feet through to the horse's head without pulling or pushing. This supportive connection encourages the horse to release his poll.

3.18 A–D *Slide Up/Slide Out* at a standstill: I maintain contact on the line with my left hand (A), then slightly stretch back with my left elbow while slowly sliding my right hand up the line to the halter (B & C). I slide my right hand back down, and repeat (D). Every time you *Slide Up*, make a connection with the halter, and *Slide Out*, you encourage the horse to lower his head, relax, and release at the poll, and you maintain connection on the line (see *reciprocity*, p. 8). Practice on both sides of the horse.

PROCEDURE

→ To begin *Slide Up/Slide Out,* stand at your horse's left side facing forward. The line should either be connected on both sides (as described on p. 38), or if only attached on one side of the halter, loop (in a figure eight) and gather the excess in your left hand. Leave no more than 2 feet of line between your left hand and the halter. Keep your left elbow bent as your left hand maintains contact on the line, and rest your right hand lightly on the line above your left (fig. 3.18 A).

→ Now, slightly stretch back with your left elbow and slowly *slide* your right hand on the line *up* to the halter. Pause for a few seconds with your right hand at the halter, and then *slide out* on the line to where you began (figs. 3.18 B–D).

→ At first the horse's tendency may be to follow the *Slide Out* movement with his head. Every time he starts to follow your right hand back out with his head, slide the hand back up to the halter to stabilize his head, and then add a little "stretch" on the line with your left elbow (fig. 3.19 A). This feels like you are drawing an archer's bow back between your hands—you create an *equal-and-opposing* stretch between your left elbow and right hand. This part of the sequence is called *Drawing the Bow.*

Eventually the horse will allow his head, poll, and neck to relax, soften, release, and begin stretching forward and down into contact on the line instead of turning toward you. Each time you *Draw the Bow*, pause before slowly *Sliding Out* to give the horse time to process the sensation of the exercise. When you *Slide Out* on the line, *own your elbow* and lighten your forearm by *thinking "up" through the wrist* so you have a straight line of connection between your elbow, the line, and the horse's halter (fig. 3.19 B). Continue to *Slide Up/Slide Out* several times, and then "take the horse for a walk" (see p. 59) to process the new sensations.

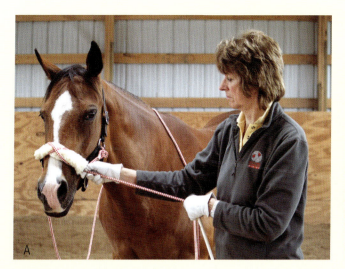 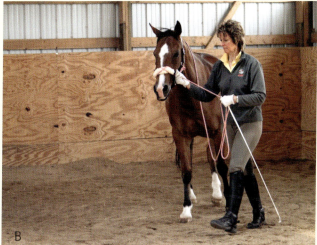

3.19 A & B To *Draw the Bow*, keep your right hand "snugged up" to the halter while your left hand provides a small "stretch" on the line (A). This exercise can be done at a standstill and in motion (B). In B, notice how straight the line is from the mare's head to my left hand. Her head is very "light" in my hands, and you can see her soft expression and focused attitude.

OBSERVATIONS

Does your horse show signs of accepting the work that's being asked? Is he accepting the contact? Does he walk with more purpose or focus when you are *Drawing the Bow*? Does he bend through the rib cage and stretch his topline as you work him from the ground? As you do this and other leading exercises, you will notice the horse's head lowering and his neck softening, as well as other signs of *release* (see p. 8). Your horse will increasingly be able to maintain connection on the line, whether standing still or walking. If the horse "disconnects" by tossing his head or becoming stiff through the neck and poll, "lighten" your arms (think "up"), pause, and/or slow down the exercise.

3 Combing the Line

PURPOSE

Combing the Line is a variation of *Slide Up/Slide Out* (p. 49). *Combing the Line* creates a steady connection and provides a rhythm that allows oscillation at the horse's poll. This exercise soothes and refocuses the horse—as well as the human!

PROCEDURE

→ Begin by *Drawing the Bow* (p. 50) with your right hand on the line "snugged up" to the halter.

→ Next *Slide Out* on the line with your right hand as your left hand travels up the line toward the halter. This alternating sliding motion is called *Combing the Line*.

→ As you continue *Combing the Line*, rotate your torso, first one way and then the other, with each stroke on the line. To have a clear, consistent connection with the horse, there should be no slack in the line. Remember to stay in *Neutral Posture*, "lighten" your arms, and *own your elbows*.

3.20 A–D I begin *Combing the Line* with my right hand "snugged up" to the halter and my left hand *Sliding Out* as I rotate my torso left (A). I begin to slide my right hand out as my left hand lets go of the line in preparation for changing hand position (B). My right hand continues to *Slide Out* as my left hand goes up to the halter (C). Remember to rotate your torso with each stroke on the line. When my left hand is "snugged up" to the halter, my right hand has reached its lowest point, completing the cycle (D). Notice that my right hand is even with my left elbow—the ideal distance to comb.

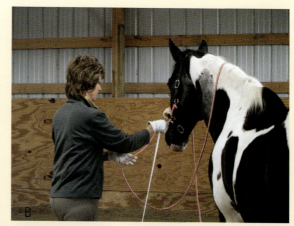
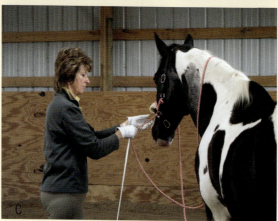
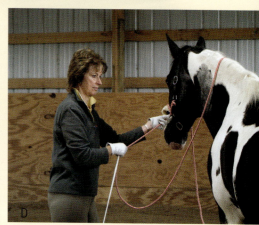

OBSERVATIONS

Horses always seem soothed by this exercise. They generally lower their head, start licking and chewing, and become "soft" in their expression. If you notice any *disconnection* in the horse's response, *think "up" through the wrists* and check your body position and your breathing. Are you holding your breath? Are you in *Neutral Posture*, or are you arched or slumped? Review the exercises in Part II (p. 19) to remind your body of its best position for encouraging connection with your horse.

4   Step to the Offside

PURPOSE

Step to the Offside invites the horse to *release* his head and neck as he takes a step, "loosening" his front feet prior to walking forward without bracing. This is a difficult task for many horses because they usually retract the neck and brace against movement when asked to walk forward. For a horse to move freely, he has to "soften" at the poll and the base of the neck, and learn to shift weight off the leg that takes the first stride forward. Eventually, when the horse learns how to release his head and neck in the first stride, it changes the quality, freedom, and energy of those that follow.

PROCEDURE

→❘ Begin on the horse's left side, facing him, and *Draw the Bow* (p. 50).

→❘ Take one *Step to the Offside* with your right foot (fig. 3.21 A). This turns the horse's head to the right and helps him take the weight off his left shoulder, allowing him to easily move his left foot. Take several more *Steps to the Offside*, guiding the horse's head slightly to the right in a smooth arc as you remain even with his head. Repeat this exercise from the right side.

→❘ If the horse is stiff or doesn't want to move, simplify the exercise by taking just one *Step to the Offside*, then stop, *Slide Out* on the line, and let your horse process (see p. 7). Or, start by *Sliding Out* and *Combing the Line*; then take one or two steps *backward* to loosen the horse's hind end, before then taking a *Step to the Offside* (fig. 3.21 B).

→❘ Now "take your horse for a walk" with the line held in a relaxed manner, so he can process (see p. 59). By breaking this exercise down into small steps, your horse will get used to the idea of walking off to either side while maintaining connection. He will begin to lower and "soften" his head and neck and easily walk with contact on a straight line, as well as a circle.

OBSERVATIONS

When first attempting this exercise, you may find that your horse stiffens, raises his head, and braces at the poll. Some horses may refuse to move in one direction, or they begin backing up, while others try to rush forward. The reason for these reactions is that when you *Slide Up, Draw the Bow,* and *Step to the Offside*, the horse has to "let go" in places he normally braces when walking. This becomes very obvious during this exercise. Providing *your* body is not tense, you will usually see major changes in your horse's response by the second time your work on this series of exercises (fig. 3.22).

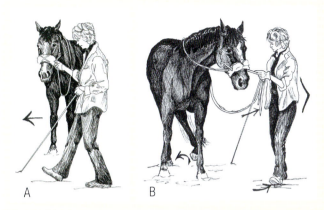

A   B

3.21 A & B Begin by *Drawing the Bow* (p. 50) to prepare the horse for *Step to the Offside.* When on the horse's left side, take a step with your right foot toward the offside (A). If the horse is stiff or refuses to move, step *backward* several steps as you *Slide Out* on the line, and then try *Stepping to the Offside* again (B). *Note:* The wand is depicted only to show the direction the handler's feet must go.

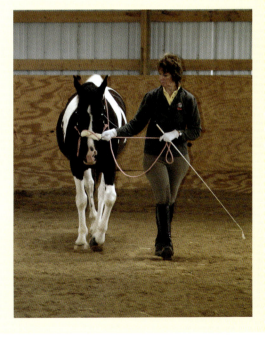

3.22 Putting it all together: Walking in connection helps the horse release his poll and "telescope" his neck, which in turn "unsticks" his front feet and enables him to walk off without bracing. This is what we're looking for—the end result of doing all the exercises in this section.

I have found that most horses step off readily to the right when you are standing on their left side, but when turning left to change direction, they may stop, raise their head, back up, speed up, or slow down. Similarly,

Noticing Connection: Feel the Oscillating Rhythm

When walking in *Neutral Posture* beside your horse, notice how your body moves with a gentle oscillating rhythm. This rhythm comes up from your feet, through your body, and is transmitted to your horse from your hands through the lead line. When you are leading in connection, this oscillation moves from human to horse, and horse to human.

Remember to Remember

As you halt with your horse, think of your arm as a light, supportive lever that helps the horse rebalance into the downward transition. When you *think "up" through the wrist,* your forearm and wrist act as a single unit. This prevents your wrist from bending in any one direction. Instead, you engage your forearm muscles as if you are getting ready to counter a downward pressure on your forearm. *Owning your elbows* engages your upper arm and shoulder muscles, primarily the triceps, to minutely stretch the elbows back. When these two movements occur simultaneously, they offer the horse a clear supportive boundary to stop. Soon you will be able to ask him to halt with an imperceptibly light "up and back" motion of your arm.

when working from their right side and stepping off to the left, they will bend their neck around, raise their head, or otherwise *disconnect* rather than move their feet. These are signs of "sidedness" in the horse (a preference for going one way or the other) and will diminish as you continue doing Connected Groundwork.

▌ Halting in Connection

The transition from walk to halt is one of the most important to accomplish while maintaining a *Neutral Posture*. Many horses are taught to halt by the handler's use of body language (at liberty) or by pulling, tugging, or jerking on the lead. These practices do not guarantee the horse will stop with freedom and alignment in his body when under saddle and on contact. Learning to halt in balance and connection is key to balanced transitions under saddle.

5   Rotation to Halt

The ideal halt occurs when the horse "softens into the transition" and remains in a balanced, *Neutral Posture*—just like the human must. A horse halting in connection feels light in your hands. More often than not, however, the place most people "drop" the connection with their horse is when they ask for the halt. The horse falls onto his forehand as the handler braces or becomes heavier with her hands.

Rotation to Halt is designed to change this habit in both horse and handler. It supports the horse as he

shifts his weight off the forehand and moves into the halt from his hind end. The exercise helps the horse override habitual bracing patterns, such as raising or turning his head, "locking" his neck, or "breaking" at the second cervical vertebrae at the top of the neck (C-2), during walk-to-halt transitions. It also helps the handler become aware that pulling is not necessary.

PROCEDURE

There are several variations to this exercise. Try all of them so you can choose the best approach for your horse. Practice the exercise at a standstill before experimenting at the walk.

→ **Basic Exercise** Stand on the left side of your horse facing forward and *Draw the Bow* (p. 50) with your right hand at the halter (fig. 3.22 A). Release the stretch between your hands and slide your right hand out on the line as you rotate your body to the right 180 degrees. Your left hand now goes up to the halter and you face the horse's hindquarters (fig. 3.22 B). *Draw the Bow* again. This causes the horse to shift his weight off his inside shoulder and toward his hind end (fig. 3.22 C). The hand at the horse's head should remain straight through the wrist and light—*think "up" with your wrist*. As in other

3.22 A–C I begin the exercise facing forward and *Drawing the Bow* (A). I then rotate my body right until I face the horse's hindquarters, which shifts the horse's weight from his left foreleg to his right foreleg (B). I again *Draw the Bow* (B). This shifts the horse's weight again, and ultimately, the horse rebalances over all four legs (C).

exercises, remember to stay "soft" in your back, released in the crease at your hip joint, and flexed slightly at your knees.

Once you bring the horse to the halt, think "up and back" with your left hand and ask the horse to back up several steps. With the wand in your right hand, give a small flick on the lower part of the cannon bone of the leg you want to take a step back first. Wait for the horse to move that leg, then flick the other front leg with the wand, and again wait for a response. Then, walk the horse forward again for a few strides before repeating *Rotation to Halt.*

→ **Variation 1** As in the exercise *Topline Stretch* (p. 107), follow this procedure: Begin on the left side of the horse. *Draw the Bow* by sliding your right hand up to the halter, and then *Comb the Line* (p. 51). *Draw the Bow* again, and take one or two *Steps to the Offside* (p. 52), then pause. With your left foot take a step sideways to give yourself some distance from the horse (fig. 3.23), then *Comb the Line* as you take several steps backward until the horse's head turns toward you and his body follows. *Draw the Bow* and stop walking.

→ **Variation 2** Follow the same steps as in the Basic Exercise (p. 54). Leave your left hand at the halter while your right hand slides down the lower part of the

3.23 In *Rotation to Halt Variation 1,* take a step sideways with your outside foot to give yourself some distance from the horse before taking several steps backward and Combing the Line to the halt.

3.24 In *Rotation to Halt Variation 2,* slide your right hand (when standing on the horse's left) down the jugular groove to the base of the horse's neck and make a brief closing motion with your hand. This helps the horse shift his weight back.

3.25 In *Rotation to Halt Variation 3,* I make contact with the outside line—holding it at base of the horse's neck—to offer the horse extra support.

horse's neck with your thumb in the jugular groove (as if you are doing *Caterpillars*—p. 64—backward). When your hand reaches the base of the neck, it feels as if you have landed on a shelf (fig. 3.24). Make a momentary closing motion with your hand. This helps the horse shift his weight to his hind end in the transition. Be mindful of your own posture.

→ǀ **Variation 3** With the line connected to the halter on both sides (see p. 38), proceed with the steps in the Basic Exercise (p. 54). Prepare for a transition to the halt by making contact with the *outside* line (when standing on the horse's left, the end of the line that is connected on the right side of the halter) by grasping the loop of the line with your right hand and bringing it to the base of the horse's neck at the shoulder-chest junction as you rotate your body to face the horse's hindquarters (fig. 3.25). This provides extra support for the horse. As the downward transition occurs, your left hand at the halter should remain "light" and think "up," while the hand holding the line at the base of the neck thinks "down."

OBSERVATIONS

I am always fascinated by how horses square themselves up and consistently improve their walk as they go through the transitions introduced in this exercise. Again, the most critical aspect throughout is that the handler pay attention to her own body, staying in *Neutral Posture* during the transition from walk to halt.

PART IV

Beginning Exercises for the Horse

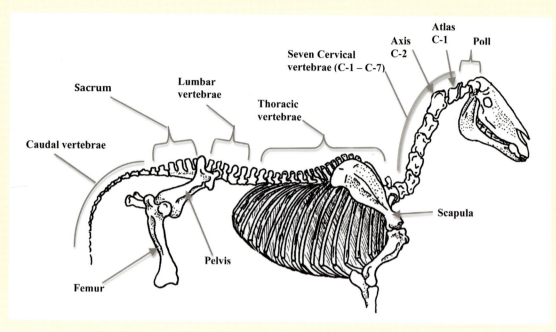

4.1 I recommend familiarizing yourself with these particular areas of the skeletal structure of the horse before beginning the core exercises in this section.

The core Connected Groundwork exercises in this section lay the foundation for unlocking habitual bracing patterns in your horse's posture. The magic of this initial group of exercises is that the horse learns to release tightness in his body and finally experience freedom of movement. He then seeks *reciprocation* (see p. 8) through connection both on the line and under saddle.

It is important for both of you to learn each of the following exercises specifically and slowly enough so they can be integrated into your complete program as you progress—think of them as a series of building blocks meant to be used in combination. I used to call these core exercises for the horse "standing still exercises" because they are initially introduced to the horse at the halt. However, once you and your horse have some proficiency, most can be done at the walk.

Before you begin, it is helpful to familiarize yourself with the basic skeletal structure of the horse (fig. 4.1). I refer to specific areas of the skeleton from time to time, and it is useful for you to already have an understanding of how the horse is "put together."

▌ Twenty-One Standing Still Exercises

1   Cheek Press

PURPOSE

Cheek Press is a way to assess if the horse can "release" his poll by moving his head laterally 1 or 2 degrees from side to side—a very minute amount, but sufficient enough to allow him to begin lowering his head. When a horse lowers his head, he starts to "soften" through his spine and shift his weight backward (from his forehand to his hind end), balancing his entire body so he is more receptive and able to respond to your requests. The *Cheek Press* literally starts the process of making sure the horse is "ready to learn." This exercise also gives you a chance to observe if your horse is relaxed or if one side of his body is more tense than the other. If the horse cannot "give" in the poll, he will not be able to release his topline, bend his rib cage, lift his back, or push from behind ("come through").

"Go for a Walk" and "Let the Horse Process"

In the exercises in this book, from time to time I instruct you to "go for a walk" and "let the horse process." This means make a small *counter* circle—with your body positioned on the *outside* of the circle and the horse on the *inside*—6 to 8 meters (20 to 26 feet) in diameter), and come back to where you started. The purpose is to give the horse a moment to process the work you have just done and to begin to feel his body in a different way. During these "breaks," do not ask the horse to do anything other than walk the circle in connection with an oscillating rhythm (see p. 6). When you walk a small circle, the horse has to be aware of his feet. This increased awareness aides in the integration process and is where he puts everything together.

It can take up to three minutes, and sometimes longer (15 or 20!) to give the horse enough time to process. Observe your horse's posture when you *Rotate to Halt* (p. 54) at the end of the walk. Usually, the horse will rebalance, "square himself up," and become quiet and peaceful, with his head and neck at withers level or lower. I call this being "in the zone." His eyes may be half shut or even closed. He is unconcerned with any activity going on around him.

If your horse is "in the zone" and you resume an exercise only to find he is not "all there," stop and take a minute or two to wait for a sign that he has come out of his meditation. He may say, "I'm here now," by taking a huge breath, or by moving a foot. If after about three minutes he still hasn't indicated that he has "reawakened," he may be saying, "I'm full of information for today"—often a good time to stop the exercise or end the groundwork session.

When starting Connected Groundwork, I advise limiting sessions to 20 minutes total or working in short increments with frequent intermissions when the horse is allowed to process. Each time you give your horse a break and "go for a walk," you will likely see an increase in his retention as well as his tolerance for learning additional material.

4.2 During the exercises ahead, periodically "go for a walk" to give the horse a moment to absorb what you have just done. As you walk a small circle, your horse "processes" and "integrates" what he has learned into his nervous system.

The object of *Cheek Press* is to apply the least amount of "press" necessary to initiate the horse "softening" in your hand and "releasing" on his own.

PROCEDURE

→ Stand on the left side of the horse facing his throatlatch. Place your left hand on the bridge of the horse's nose across the halter noseband. Make a loose fist with your right hand and place it in the center of the horse's left cheek (fig. 4.3 A). Make sure your wrist is straight to maintain connection with the horse.

→ With your left hand, invite the horse's head to come toward you, and with your right hand, suggest his cheek move away (fig. 4.3 B). This creates a very subtle *equal-and-opposing* sensation.

→ Hold this position for a few seconds, applying "1" or "2" degrees of pressure and allowing the horse to accept your hands (see sidebar, *The TTouch Pressure Scale*, on p. 60). Then increase pressure to "3" or "4," take a deep breath, and hold for five to 10 seconds (fig. 4.3 C). You want the horse's head to "soften" in your hands. Sometimes the head will yield slightly to the side or begin to lower. At this

The TTouch™ Pressure Scale

The Tellington Method's TTouch Pressure Scale goes from 1 to 10, and it was established by practitioners to help you determine the amount of pressure to apply in specific areas of a horse's body to produce particular effects. I use the same Pressure Scale in my Connected Groundwork and refer to pressure values in the exercises on the pages ahead. To help you understand how to use variations of pressure in the exercises in this book, I've included the following explanation of the TTouch Pressure Scale from Linda Tellington-Jones' book *The Ultimate Horse Behavior and Training Book* (www.horseandriderbooks.com).

→⊢ To learn the measure of each number on the Pressure Scale, begin with the lightest pressure—using "1" as a baseline. Bring your right hand up to your face, supporting your bent right elbow snugly against your body with your other hand. (Reverse if you are left-handed.) Place your thumb against your cheek to steady your hand and put the tip of your middle finger just below your eye socket, pushing the skin in a circle with the lightest possible contact—so you can feel only tissue with no hint of bone underneath—and just enough contact that you do not slide over the skin. This is a "1" pressure.

→⊢ Next, on the fleshy part of your forearm, between your wrist and your elbow, place your curved finger on top of the arm with your thumb on the underside so you hold the arm be-tween the fingers and thumb. Make a circle using the same minimal possible contact as you did on your cheekbone. Observe how little indentation you make in the skin. Register the feeling of this "1" pressure in your mind.

→⊢ To identify a "3" pressure, repeat the process, but this time push the skin in a circle with enough pressure that you feel the top of the cheekbone clearly without pushing hard. Retaining the sensorial memory of that pressure, return to your forearm and compare this slightly increased pressure to the "1" pressure. Note the difference in indentation in your skin between the "1" and "3" pressure, and the difference in the feeling.

→⊢ Now go back to your cheekbone and make a circle pressing firmly on the bone itself. Take that feeling back to your forearm and you have a "6." The indentation on your forearm will be twice as deep into the muscle with a "6" pressure. When a pressure heavier than a "6" is done with the pads of the fingers, it can cause both "doer" and "do-ee" to feel discomfort and hold her breath.

(For further information about TTouch and the Pressure Scale, see Linda Tellington-Jones' numerous books and DVDs—turn to the Recommended Reading on p. 137 or visit www.ttouch.com.)

point, either end the exercise or *slowly* increase the pressure on the cheek and nose. Take another breath and again hold for several seconds. Slowly release the pressure on the cheek, take your hands off the horse, and observe him briefly. You aren't telling the horse to turn his head—you are *suggesting* he "soften" his head in your hands and yield minutely to the left or right (fig. 4.3 D). The goal of *Cheek Press* is that the poll "softens" and the head starts to lower.

→⊢ Repeat the exercise two to four times on both sides.

→⊢ **Variation 1** If your horse won't let you touch his head or put your left hand on the bridge of his nose (when standing on his left), hold the line in your left hand about 12 inches down the line, maintaining contact as your right hand presses on the horse's cheek (fig. 4.4). I have always witnessed a positive change with this variation except when a horse has a major dental imbalance or extreme tension in the head and neck. It may take some time (weeks!) for such a horse to be able to respond positively to *Cheek Press*.

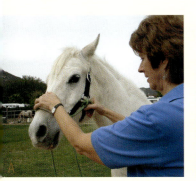

4.3 A–D Begin the *Cheek Press* with one hand on the halter noseband and the other in a soft fist on the horse's cheek (A). Here the initial response is, "I'm not so sure I want your hands on my face!" I "invite" the nose toward me and "press" the cheek away (B). Notice the difference in the horse—he's thinking, "This might not be so bad." Next I increase the pressure from a "1" or "2" to a "3" or "4" (C) and the horse's head position changes minutely as he replies, "Hmmmmm…maybe you've got something there." Finally, you see the horse "soften" in my hands (D). "Aaaah," he seems to say. "I appreciate the way my poll feels relaxed and supported."

OBSERVATIONS

Notice if the horse is more giving and flexible when you do this exercise on one side or the other. Learn to recognize what bracing patterns the horse exhibits—for instance, when you place your hands on his face, does he brace and continue bracing? Brace and then "soften"? Or soften the minute you put your hands on him, as if he were melting into you?

You may feel the horse's head soften under your hands or the cheek yield to your fist—this is what you are looking for, to do the least amount to get the horse to *release*. The horse's head may drop, his eyes may start to close, and his gaze may become tranquil. Sometimes the nostrils flare or the horse takes a deep breath. Occasionally, the horse shakes his head and neck, or his entire body, and lets out a big snort. His lower lip may seem to tremble, his whiskers wiggle, or his nostrils may drip.

Oftentimes *nothing* happens… *until* you take your hands away, and then *any* of these signs may occur.

It may happen that as you increase pressure on the horse's cheek, he pulls away, raises his head, or plunges it downward. Or he may back up when you begin to press. He may be reluctant to accept your hands on his face. These are all signs of bracing and extreme tight-

4.4 Cheek Press Variation 1 helps deal with a horse that does not tolerate your hand over the bridge of his nose. Instead you can hold the line about 12 inches away from the head and "press" the cheek while walking.

ness, or they may indicate temporomandibular joint (TMJ) stiffness, dental problems, or chiropractic issues in the neck.

If the horse does not "release" or if his negative response to the exercise is really intense, give him time to think about it by going for a brief walk (see p. 59), switch sides, move on to another exercise, or try again another day.

> ## Remember to Remember
>
> When a horse appears not to "like" an exercise, there is usually an underlying physical reason, or the person handling him is tense and not in *Neutral Posture*. The issue may be resolved by going on to different exercises before returning to the one in question, and the handler should check her position. Your goal is to find exercises in which the horse feels safe and demonstrates trust, comfort, and "release."
>
> Sometimes a horse requires additional therapeutic support such as chiropractic, massage, or the Tellington Method.

2   Cheek Delineation

PURPOSE

Cheek Delineation is another exercise to improve mobility and flexibility in the poll area and ensure that its movement from side to side is equal. It can help horses with tension in the temporomandibular joint (TMJ) as well as those that have been "held" in a frame or ridden in training "gadgets" (such as running or German martingales). *Cheek Delineation* is also beneficial for horses that have thickness in the throatlatch area due to swollen glands, overdeveloped neck muscles, dental problems, or conformational issues.

PROCEDURE

→ Stand on the left side of the horse facing his throatlatch. Place your left hand on the line and "snug it up" to the halter (see p.42). Place the index, middle, and ring fingers of your right hand in the groove just below the horse's ear, behind the cheekbone, and slowly trace (*delineate*) the groove downward, following the outline of the cheekbone (fig. 4.5 A). Use no more "2" to "3" degrees of pressure (see p. 60), and keep your hand slightly cupped. It feels like your fingertips are hooking onto the edge of the cheekbone and tracing its outer edge.

→ Repeat this movement two or three times, and let the horse process the sensation (figs. 4.5 B & C). If there are areas that seem thicker or harder to the touch, slow down or remain in that spot for a few seconds, lightening your touch. About halfway down the groove, for example, there are salivary and lymph glands, and you may encounter congestion (thickening or hardening) due to tension in the poll and upper neck area. *Cheek Delineation* helps relieve this congestion.

→ Once the horse has "softened" in the throatlatch area, remind his nervous system of its natural ability to release laterally at the poll by pressing the *midpoint* of the outer line of the cheekbone (fig. 4.6). This suggests to the horse he can yield his head in either direction. The midpoint is the place where the horse's head can swing sideways with the most freedom. If this area is free of tension, the horse is better able to bend throughout his body.

→ Once your horse has accepted this exercise at the standstill, try it at the walk (fig. 4.7). This is a great way to remind the horse at any time to let go of tension in this area.

OBSERVATIONS

As the horse "releases" during this exercise, you may see any of the following: lowered head; lateral yielding of the poll; licking; chewing; taking a deep breath; flared nostrils; wiggling whiskers; closed eyes; and increased focus. Take the horse for a walk and look for differences in gait, such as freer movement. Sometimes in the process of doing an exercise, it might not seem like much of anything is happening, but once the horse is taken for a walk and allowed time to process, his movement will subsequently improve and he will display a greater aptitude for relaxing and learning.

When the horse is uncomfortable with the exercise, he may pull his head away, lose focus, back up, or fidget.

4.5 A–C I begin *Cheek Delineation* with my left hand on the line "snugged up" to the halter. This horse's initial response to the exercise is to become tense and anxious—he has raised and tilted his head away (A). If your horse objects to your touch, delineate the cheek groove very lightly (with a "1" to "2" pressure). After a brief pause, I delineate the horse's cheek again, and this time he accepts the contact and maintains the connection while I slide my hand out on the line (B). After a few *Cheek Delineations*, he stretches his neck and lowers his head, clearly enjoying the new sensations of lightness and freedom (C).

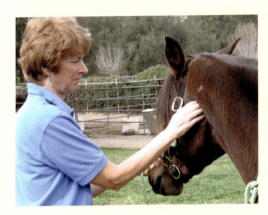

4.7 You can do *Cheek Delineation* at the walk by softly cupping your fingertips around the horse's cheekbone.

4.6 Placing my fingers at the midpoint of the cheek helps this horse rotate his head and neck laterally with ease.

If this is the case, give the horse a chance to process, try the exercise on the other side, and/or proceed to another exercise. You can always come back to *Cheek Delineation*. If the horse settles and focuses, you are on the right track.

Remember to Remember

If your horse gets "stuck," try something else—go for a walk, do nothing for 30 seconds, switch sides, or change exercises. Give your horse time to absorb what he has learned with a short break.

3 Caterpillar

PURPOSE

Caterpillar promotes "telescoping" of the horse's neck—release of the poll, opening of the throatlatch, lifting of the base of the neck, and freedom through the shoulders—both at a standstill and walk. *Caterpillar* helps horses stretch into contact and yield to the line or reins through turns.

PROCEDURE

→ Stand on the horse's left side, facing his neck. "Snug up" your left hand to the halter while maintaining lightness by *thinking "up" through the wrist*. Alternatively, you can hook your left index, left index and middle fingers, or thumb in front of the "T" junction of the halter's noseband near the lower side ring (figs. 4.8 A & B). The purpose of hooking the fingers is to maintain connection and steady the horse's head, but use common sense and be prepared to remove your fingers quickly should your horse startle.

→ Place your right hand on the base of the horse's neck above the point of the shoulder (fig. 4.9 A). In the steps that follow, your thumb traces the jugular groove as the rest of your fingers rest at the top ridge of the vertebrae at the base of the horse's neck. It feels as if you are cupping your hand around the vertebrae, with your fingers pointing toward the horse's ears (fig. 4.9 B). Hold the heel of your hand in a clamshell shape, so the outer edge of your whole hand is in contact with the horse.

→ Move your right hand up the neck in four steps. First, slide your hand up with your thumb following the jugular groove, your hand "cupped" around the vertebrae, and your fingers pointing toward the horse's ears. Repeat this motion while relaxing and lightening your left hand on the halter.

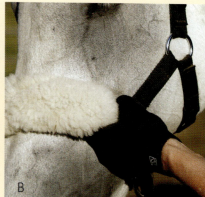

4.8 A & B Grasp the "T" junction of the halter's noseband either with your index and middle fingers (A) or—when your horse is "heavy" with his head—with your thumb (B). Your forearm and wrist must remain light and thinking "up."

→ Second, slide up the neck toward the horse's left ear focusing on "pressing" from the heel of your hand. Practice smooth, connected movements with "2" to "4" degrees of pressure (see the TTouch Pressure Scale, p. 60).

→ Third, slide your hand up the neck, allowing your fingers to plough slowly through the horse's coat with "2" to "4" degrees of pressure.

→ Finally, put it all together: Starting again at the base of the neck, slowly open and close your hand as you slide it up the neck. Think of your hand as a caterpillar inching up the neck, vertebra by vertebra. As the heel of your hand presses and moves toward the ears, allow your fingers to plough through the horse's coat with a "closing" and "opening" motion toward your thumb. Slightly cup your hand and fingers during the movement and use "2" to "4" degrees of pressure. Repeat this exercise four to five times and give the horse time to process in between (figs. 4.10 A & B).

→ *Caterpillar* can be done at the walk with your left hand slid out about 12 inches on the line (figs. 4.11 A–C). *Caterpillar* at the walk helps the horse let go of bracing patterns and release the base of his neck.

4.9 A & B Begin the *Caterpillar* exercise with your hand placed at the base of the horse's neck (A). If the horse is tense, be very light with your touch. The placement of your hand "cups" the neck vertebrae as you start *Caterpillar* up the neck (B). Your hand follows the path of the vertebrae from the base of the shoulder to the poll.

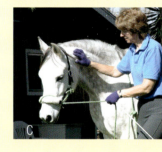

4.11 A–C *Caterpillar* can be practiced at the walk with one hand slid out about 12 inches on the line. Note the progressive lowering and "telescoping" of this horse's head and neck in these three photos.

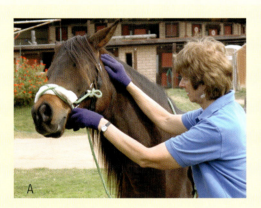 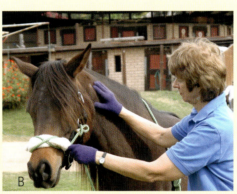

4.10 A & B If the horse reacts with tension or anxiety to your touch at the top of the neck, stop the exercise, take the horse for a walk, let him process, and try *Caterpillar* again—or move to a different exercise (A). After a pause, I do *Caterpillar* again with this horse and this time she responds by lowering her head and beginning to accept the exercise (B).

OBSERVATIONS

The horse's head lowers, the neck "telescopes," the eyes "soften," the mouth relaxes, the nostrils flare, and sometimes the horse takes a big breath or snorts. Oftentimes after going for a walk and then coming back to a halt, the horse will stand more squarely and calmly.

When the horse is tense, his head might come up, or he may move away from you, back up, or try to nip or bite as your hand moves up his neck. Lighten your pressure and simplify the exercise (softly pass your hand up the neck), and if this does not release the horse's tension or gain his trust, stop what you are doing. Take the horse for a short walk to allow him to process, then try again, work on the opposite side, or move on to another exercise.

Remember to Remember

If the horse acts like he is uncomfortable, slow down and think "up" through your wrists, shoulders, elbows, and hands. If the horse's head is lower and he seems more peaceful after the exercise, you are on the right track.

Case Study: ROSE

with Connected Riding Instructors Jillian Kreinbring and Lindsay Cummings

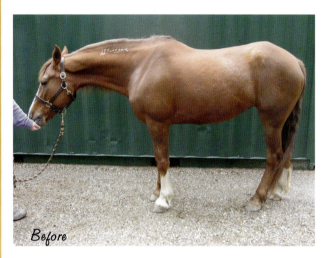

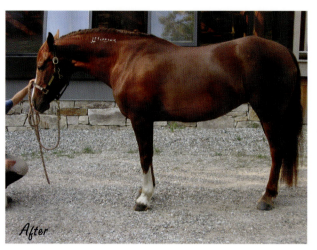

Study Length
Ten months

Background
Rose is a 15-year-old Mustang mare. She was taken from the range at three months of age, started Western, sold, and placed into dressage training where she was trained and competed to third level before we bought her.

Presenting Issue
When Rose came into the Connected Groundwork and Connected Riding program, she was shut down physically and mentally. In the arena and on the trails, she would often spook and spin. While working in the arena, she was mechanical in her movements, showed no expression, and was extremely "heavy" in hand and under saddle. Rose was pushed as a youngster and was not physically strong enough to perform many of the dressage movements she was asked for, so she learned to compensate in her body, straining her lumbosacral region and becoming very tight and unyielding at the poll.

Process
The first thing we did was turn Rose out with a herd on pasture. For the first two months, we did only Connected Groundwork an average of four times a week for 30 minutes at a time as to not overwhelm her system. We did mostly *Caterpillar, Cheek Press, Cheek Delineation, Shoulder Delineation, Spine Rock, Belly Lifts,* and *Tail Rocks* at the halt. At the walk, we did *Slide-Up/Slide-Out, Shoulder Press, Heart-Girth Press, Draw the Bow, Walking "S" One-Hand* and *Two-Hands,* as well as many hours of *Connected Longeing.* At the end of each session we would take her for a walk in the pasture where we focused on *Walking "S"* curves and using Tellington Method leading positions: *Elegant Elephant, Dingo, Cueing the Camel,* and *Grace of the Cheetah* (see p. 137). We were looking for the constant release of Rose's topline and relaxation of her poll.

As Rose became more interested and curious about her work sessions, we started riding her on the trails. Before each ride we would do 15 minutes of groundwork to assess Rose's body and to release any tension we might find. During our rides, we looked for the same reactions under saddle as we did when doing Connected Groundwork. We rode Rose up and down hills at the walk and worked on lateral movements. We again focused on the release of her poll. As the tension started to melt away, we asked Rose for increased energy from the hindquarters and began trotting up hills. We were always mindful of Rose's attempts to stretch into contact.

After about eight months, we began riding Rose in the arena for very short periods. We wanted to continue on our positive path by not overwhelming her with mechanical exercises in the ring. We used Connected Groundwork for a warmup, rode for 20 minutes in the arena where we worked on stretching and lateral movements, and finished on the trails trotting up and down hills. At this point, Rose consistently began flexing her hindquarters, using her abdominals, basculing her back, and "telescoping" her neck into a light connection.

Currently Rose is strong and relaxed enough through her body to work on collected movements. She is rarely "heavy" in the hand or on the bridle, and has never spooked or spun on the trail or in the arena. She has let go of a significant amount of tension in her poll and no longer moves in a mechanical way. We have a great deal of fun together and we are so very grateful to Connected Groundwork and the Tellington Method for giving us tools to build a healthy, loving relationship with Rose.

4 Shoulder Delineation

PURPOSE

Shoulder Delineation helps horses release tightness in the shoulders that hinders their ability to lengthen stride, "telescope" their neck, turn freely, and move laterally. It helps horses shift their weight dynamically from side to side, from base down to base up (see p. 2), and from forehand to haunches. *Shoulder Delineation* is particularly useful when horses have a difficult time stopping or have steep shoulders, which predisposes them to tension and overdeveloped shoulder muscles. It is also beneficial to use this exercise when a horse has been hauled a long distance in a trailer or if he is stall-bound.

PROCEDURE

→ Stand on the horse's left side facing forward with your left hand positioned on the halter or about 12 inches down the line. Rotate your body slightly to the left and fold (crease) at your hip (see p. 32) while placing your right-hand fingers at the top of the horse's shoulder just below the withers in front of the scapula (see fig. 4.1, p. 58). Curve your fingers together and point them downward, then follow the groove that begins in front of the shoulder blade, slowly traveling down along its edge (figs. 4. 13 A & B).

→ Often, when you begin *Shoulder Delineation* at the top of the scapula, the groove is tight and barely visible. As you move along the shoulder, you can trace (delineate) it more deeply, and then, as you approach the point of the shoulder, the groove may again become less defined and feel less accessible. To help the horse relax and open the *Shoulder Delineation* area, place your left hand at the "T"-junction of the halter's lower side ring and slowly rotate your body left while following the groove with your right hand (fig. 4.14). As you rotate, the horse's head will come toward you and your fingers will go deeper into the groove as he shifts his weight off the near shoulder.

4.13 A & B To do a *Shoulder Delineation*, follow the groove of the shoulder with the outside edge of your hand, with your fingers curled and pointed down (A). You will almost have a sense of "slicing" through the muscle. After some time to process, followed by a few more *Shoulder Delineations,* this horse lowers his head, "softens" his eye, and maintains connection on the line (B).

→ Try this exercise at the walk (figs. 4.15 A & B). You can delineate the shoulder by placing your arm in the scapular groove as you move beside your horse.

OBSERVATIONS

As the horse lets go of tension and releases, you will see signs of acceptance and relaxation, and he may begin to lower his head and "telescope" his neck. Notice if one shoulder is easier to delineate than the other. The horse may object by backing up, tossing his head, nipping, twitching his skin, or moving away. These are all signs of tightness and tension in the shoulders. Slow your movements and lighten your touch; try delineating on his other side, or take the horse for a brief walk before returning to the exercise.

Signs of bracing or tightness are common in this area, and the groove in the shoulder may at first seem nearly impenetrable. But even when the horse objects to the exercise, you may notice his walk becomes freer, he stops more readily, and he stands differently afterward.

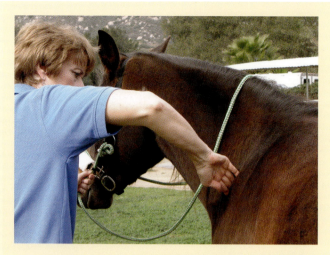

4.14 Keeping your fingers pointing down as you delineate the shoulder helps you get into the scapular groove, which may be tight when you begin this exercise.

4.15 A & B Horses love doing *Shoulder Delineation* at the walk. It encourages them to stretch their head and neck down and bend through their rib cage. In these photos I'm delineating the shoulder by placing my forearm in the shoulder groove.

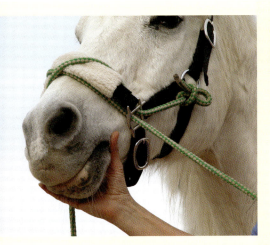

4.16 Gently cup your hand under your horse's chin, offering to "meet" the weight of the horse's head and help support it. This horse is actually resting his head in my hand.

4.17 A & B *Chin Rest* at the walk helps horses release tension in their head and neck, especially when they have been worked or ridden in an overflexed position. Here you can see my position from two different angles.

Over time, I have found this exercise helps the shoulder area soften, and it becomes much easier to delineate.

5 Chin Rest

PURPOSE

Chin Rest relieves tension in the poll and upper regions of the neck. It also helps reeducate horses that tend to go behind the vertical by encouraging them to open their throatlatch and stretch into contact.

PROCEDURE

→| Stand on the left side of the horse at his head, facing forward. Gently cup your right hand under the horse's chin groove and "meet" the weight of his head in your hand (fig. 4.16). Hold the line with your left hand no more than 2 feet from his head. Support the weight of the head in your right hand for 10 to 90 seconds—longer if the horse is showing signs of relaxation by closing his eyes and "giving you"

his head to hold. Make sure you support the head, but do not lift it, as that would invert (hollow) the horse's neck. And remember that a horse's head can get heavy, so make sure you "unlock" your knees and stay "soft" in your back and hips.

→| Next, slowly release the weight of the head from your hand. Allow the horse to process before repeating the exercise two to four times. When the horse is comfortable with the exercise, he will willingly rest the weight of his head in your hand.

→| Try the exercise at the walk (figs. 4.17 A & B). It is important for you to have a connection on the line, a "crease" in your hip joint, and a "soft" back as you move in *Neutral Posture*. Walk beside the horse in *Chin Rest* for 8 to 10 strides and then give the horse time to process while *Combing the Line* (p. 51). A wonderful addition is to add a few steps of *Caterpillar* (see p. 64).

OBSERVATIONS

Ask yourself the following questions as you observe your

4.18 A & B Here are two examples of "stuck" feet. When a horse has been worked on the forehand, his feet often get "stuck" during a change of direction since his base does not shift from down to up (see p. 2). I find that many horses initially respond this way during a change of direction while *Walking "S" One Hand* (p. 102).

horse: Does he toss his head? Is his head "heavy" or "light" (see p. 5)? After repeating the exercise several times, does his behavior change? Does the horse stretch his head and neck down when you slowly stop supporting his chin? Is the horse able to stand still while you do this exercise?

When a horse has a lot of stiffness in the neck and poll, he may react to this exercise in two ways. If he typically raises his head when he is anxious or during transitions, he may not accept contact under the chin at all. Or he may accept contact but not release his head, which means you will be supporting ounces of weight instead of pounds. In the latter scenario, lifting his head just a fraction, invites the horse to begin to let his head go.

If the horse backs away, drops his back, or tosses his head, stop what you are doing, go for a short walk, and observe whether the horse's head is lower and his walk freer as he moves—despite his objections to the exercise. Then try the exercise again or return to it another day.

A horse that accepts the exercise shows the usual signs of relaxation: closing his eyes and seeming sleepy, taking a deep breath, flaring his nostrils, letting out a good snort, or shaking his neck or entire body. When you slowly release the weight of the horse's head, it often lowers farther than it was before, and frequently

the horse stretches his head and neck all the way to the ground. As the horse stretches downward, be sure to maintain light contact but allow the line to slide through your fingers.

In some cases a horse's head is quite heavy and you cannot hold it up for long—it will feel as if the horse is pushing down on your hand. I have experienced this with cribbers and other horses that have undue tension in the head and neck, perhaps from being forced into a frame and ridden behind the vertical. These horses can actually "lighten" in the head area, and their posture will change as you continue with the other Connected Groundwork exercises, particularly *Caterpillar* (p. 64).

6   The "V"

PURPOSE

We are moving out of the first set of exercises that focus on the head and neck, into exercises that help the horse lift his thoracic sling (a combination of muscles and ligaments that suspend the chest and work as a shock absorber for the front end of the horse during movement), free his rib cage so it can bend, and "soften" the back so it can "swing."

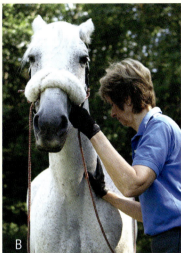

4.19 A–C As the horse's shoulder groove softens and widens, notice that the horse shifts his weight to the offside (A). This horse shows signs of tension as I begin to work up the base of his neck, but he "softens" as I continue the lifting motion with my hand (B & C).

The purpose of *The "V"* is to aid horses that tend to plant their feet and get "stuck"—not readily moving or shifting their weight when asked to go forward (figs. 4.18 A & B). Getting "stuck" indicates tension and habitual bracing. It is almost as if nerve impulses from the brain are not making it to the feet. Such horses often display lack of forward motion, dullness to the aids, stumbling, and an inclination to travel on the forehand with no bend in their body.

The "V" is also useful with the extremely stiff horse that turns like a large boat (without any bend through the body) as well as the horse that finds it almost impossible to shift his weight efficiently; the horse that "rubber-necks"; the large horse that tends to plant his front feet; the horse that is difficult to stop; and the horse with an upside-down (ewe) neck.

PROCEDURE

→ *The "V"* is an abbreviated form and combination of *Caterpillar* (p. 64) and *Shoulder Delineation* (p. 67). Start by standing at the horse's left side facing the point where the neck and shoulder meet. Hold the line in your left hand "snugged up" to the halter. Trace the last 4 inches of the path from the *Shoulder Delineation* exercise using a "2" or "3" pressure (see p. 60) with your right hand. Gradually increase the pressure and allow your body to rotate left as your fingers delineate the shoulder groove. The goal is for the horse to shift his weight from the left front foot to the right front foot and begin bending through the body. As you follow the groove with your fingers, it should become softer and wider, and you may notice the horse shifts his weight (fig. 4.19 A). Repeat four to six times and allow the horse time to process. Take note of positive responses, such as lowering of the head and an audible big sigh.

→ Continue with this exercise by doing the first 4 inches of *Caterpillar*. Begin with a "2" to "3" pressure and gradually increase it, as if you are suggesting to the horse that he let his neck lengthen outward, just as a turtle lets his head out of a shell. The "lifting" effect of your hand as you rotate your torso to the right encourages the horse to also rotate to the right and so move his left front leg. Eventually, the left front leg will cross in front of the right. This exercise may require repetition over a number of days.

→ Now combine the two movements by sliding down to the end of the shoulder groove (the last 4 inches)

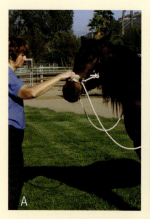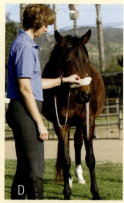

4.20 A–F In this series of photos I am *Tracing the Arc* with a mare who had a lot of tension in her head and neck. I begin facing her, with my right finger hooked over the halter noseband (A). I take one step to the left and the mare releases her head and neck. Notice that from the second photo (B) to the third photo (C) there is about an inch difference in the position of her head as she progressively lowers it. The mare is relaxed and her eye is "soft" as I switch positions and *Trace the Arc* in the other direction (D & E). She gives smoothly in tiny increments, signifying the neck is releasing and bending. In addition, her weight shifts, and she is relaxed as I complete the exercise in the other direction (F).

while rotating your torso to the left, then immediately move up the neck while rotating to the right (about 4 inches). Your fingers trace the imaginary pattern of the letter "V" (figs. 4.19 B & C).

Note: Some horses respond better if you reverse the order of the movements.

OBSERVATIONS

Anytime a horse objects to the amount of pressure you are using, lighten it until he is more comfortable with what you are doing. You may have to begin with one part of the exercise before gradually adding the remaining elements—and this may take several sessions over a period of days.

After practicing this exercise, you may notice that a horse that *wasn't* taking contact now does so on the line, and a horse that was "heavy" on the line becomes lighter.

7 Tracing the Arc

PURPOSE

Tracing the Arc enables the horse to free up his range of motion from the base of his neck to his poll, while at the same time shifting weight off the forehand and onto the hind end. It also encourages the horse to bend through his body in an arc and prepares him to let his head and neck release as he walks. This is a very slow, nonhabitual exercise that gives the horse time to process, shift his weight, and relax the muscles of the poll, topline, and neck. It improves the horse's ability to accept contact under saddle while rebalancing and changing direction, as well as during upward and downward transitions.

PROCEDURE

→ Begin by facing the horse's head (this is the center of the imaginary arc you will trace with the horse's nose). Lightly hook your right index finger just to the right of center on the halter's noseband (your

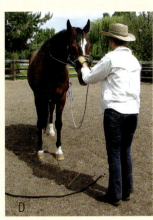

4.21 A–D Another view of *Tracing the Arc*, showing me take several steps to the right with a lead rope on the ground for a visual.

left hand is free) and take one step to your left, suggesting that the horse follow your motion (figs. 4.20 A–C). Pause and let the horse "soften" his head into your hand.

→ Change hands, placing your left index finger just to the left of center on the noseband. Slowly take one step to the right, back to the center of your imaginary arc (where you started). Pause and again allow the horse to "soften" into your hand.

→ Now take one step to the right of the middle of your imaginary arc (figs. 4.20 D–F). Repeat. Once the horse can respond quietly in each direction, try taking more than one step to the left and to the right, pausing for a release with each new step as you *Trace the Arc* (figs. 4.21 A–D). At first you may only be able to move a couple of steps in one direction before your horse becomes "stuck." Remember to relax your knees, hips, and back, keeping your arm light.

→ *Note:* When this exercise is done at the walk, it becomes part of *Walking "S" One Hand* (p. 102).

OBSERVATIONS

When the horse is tense or braced, he may toss his head, back up, "make faces," become mouthy, or act head shy. Some horses are unable to release in one direction and will let you know with one of these reactions. Should this occur, change direction, ask for less, or allow more time for the horse to process (that is, slow down). Anytime you feel such resistance from the horse, it can really help to stop the exercise for a minute and go for a walk—then start over. Remember, the horse is not trying to be disobedient; he is just as yet unable to let go of tension in his head and neck.

Remember to Remember

With *Tracing the Arc*, it is the *stepping sideways movement* with one of your hands offering "feather light" connection to the halter that directs and suggests movement to the horse's head and neck. *Do not* use your hand to push or pull the horse. Ask him to move from the base of his neck, following the direction of your steps.

Stiff or tense horses may respond on the first step of the arc and then disconnect by losing focus on the next step. When this happens, pause and allow the horse time to process. For some horses, the first step of *Tracing the Arc* and "softening" into your hand is enough for one session. You may also find that a horse can initially only do the exercise in one direction.

With practice, the horse progressively releases with each step along the arc, he feels "light" in your hand, and he stays focused on you. He can "give" with his head and neck easily. The head feels as if there is a ball bearing in the poll area, enabling it to move smoothly in all directions.

Your horse's range of neck motion increases with each incremental release. However, *do not force the motion by taking steps without his neck releasing.* You will know he is released when his head lowers to the level of his withers, his neck stretches forward, his nostrils flare, and his eyes get that "dreamy" look.

If the horse seriously objects to the exercise, return to it later. When the horse displays major tension in the head and neck, this exercise is very difficult until that tension is released. Returning to previous Connected Groundwork exercises—such as *Caterpillar* (p. 64) and *Chin Rest* (p. 69)—can help.

8 Elephant's Trunk

PURPOSE

Elephant's Trunk helps the horse "soften" his topline so he can lift the base of his neck and "telescope" into contact. The goal of this exercise is for the horse's head and neck to move smoothly and evenly from left to right as a unit. This is another slow, nonhabitual exercise that helps the horse override bracing patterns and learn to shift the weight in his front feet more efficiently. It improves transitions and the horse's acceptance of contact under saddle. Elephant's Trunk is also great for a horse that has a hard time standing still.

The difference between *Tracing the Arc* (p. 72) and *Elephant's Trunk* is that in *Tracing the Arc,* the head turns and the neck bends, differentiating movement in each cervical vertebra. In *Elephant's Trunk,* the head

and neck remain straight and work as a unit—the movement originates at the base of the neck and the shoulders. Both exercises feel like you are not doing much—they are subtle, but their effects can be quite profound.

PROCEDURE

→ Stand at the horse's head on his left side. With your right hand "snugged up" to the halter and the rest of the line in your left hand, *Draw the Bow* (p. 49). The horse's head and neck should be straight as you begin to very slowly open your arm and send the horse's head away from your body (figs. 4.22 A–E). As you do this, let the line slide through your left hand.

→ Next, *very slowly* close your arm and bring the horse's head and neck back to their starting point (figs. 4.22 F & G). Allow your torso to rotate slightly in the direction you are opening and closing your arm—to the right as his head goes away and to the left as it comes back. This is a slow and subtle exercise—an observer might notice your arm is either closer or further away from your body, but she will not actually see you moving it. What she would notice is the connection between you and the horse.

OBSERVATIONS

Take the time to refine the smoothness of this movement. See how far you can go without the horse *disconnecting*—losing focus; moving a foot; or raising, tossing, or cocking his head. If the horse disconnects, stop for a few moments. When you resume, slow the exercise or change the direction of movement (i.e., if you are sending the head away, bring it toward you instead, and vice versa). Remember to give the horse time to process the information either by pausing or going for a walk.

Sometimes when you ask the horse to try this exercise the day following your first attempt, you will be pleasantly surprised to find him responding with ease and enjoyment. The horse may also display quiet focus throughout the exercise. His head may be lower or his

4.22 A–G Beginning *Elephant's Trunk*: My right hand is "snugged up" to the halter and my left holds the line (A). I very slowly send the horse's head away in a smooth, light, continuous movement—the contact in my hand is light and my arm is thinking "up" (B). As my arm extends my body slightly rotates to follow the movement to avoid pushing the horse's head; notice that in each photo my elbow is progressively further away from my rib cage (C & D). The mare's head is at its furthest point away from me when my arm is the most extended (E). As I bring her head back toward me, she "releases" the base of the neck, lowers her head, and has a more peaceful, mellow expression (F). I send the mare's head away once again (G). Notice how her head his lower, her neck appears longer than it did at the start of the exercise, and her eyes are starting to close. You may notice other signs of relaxation, such as flared nostrils, or licking and chewing as your horse becomes more "present."

transitions into the walk and halt lighter. You may also find that his walk has improved.

If you have a horse that reacts by throwing or "twisting" his head—perhaps even grabbing at the line, running off, or otherwise "exploding"—it is likely due to tension in the poll and neck and even in the area surrounding the cranial (head) bones. A horse like this is so out of balance he cannot even feel his own front feet. Ask for less and really slow it down. Open and close your arm no more than 3 or 4 inches. Eventually you may be able to fully extend your arm.

Case Study: ACE

with Connected Riding Instructor Trisha Wren

Before

After

Study Length

One month

Background

Ace is a four-year-old Hanoverian gelding. He was backed when he was three and ridden on the farm for about six weeks before injuring himself in the paddock and being turned out for the winter.

Presenting Issue

Ace was a young, green, unbalanced horse. He got easily distracted and tended to hold his head quite high, hollowing his back. He was often out of balance, very stiff in turns, and "heavy" in the hand, so his owner sent him to me to teach him about connection and softness.

Process

For the first two weeks I did only Connected Groundwork with Ace; I worked with him about five times a week, for about 40 minutes each session. I began at a standstill, doing a variety of exercises to improve his attention, body awareness, and ability to release tension, including *Cheek Press, Cheek Delineation, Chin Rest, Caterpillar, Drawing the Bow, Shoulder Delineation, Wither Rock, Spine Rock, Heart-Girth Press, Sacral Rock,* and *Pelvic Tilts*. From the Tellington Method toolbox I added *Back Lifts* and *Tail TTouches*.

Ace responded to these exercises quickly, lowering his head, "softening" his eyes and his body, and adjusting his posture and balance. I then introduced him to work at the walk, including *Walking "S," Drawing the Bow, Shoulder Press, Caterpillar,* and *Heart-Girth Press*.

Once Ace was able to walk while releasing and re-balancing, I introduced one-line *Connected Longeing* work. He was incredibly heavy to start with, particularly going to the right. He improved quite quickly in his walk, stretching and releasing, and stepping nicely under himself. In trot it took a few sessions for him to figure out how to release at the faster pace; I did lots of changes of rotation and *Combing the Line*. One month on, he is trotting with lovely elevation and stretch to the right, though still "motor-biking" a little to the left. Ace's body has filled out and rounded, and he rarely lifts his head high. His back and hindquarters have strengthened and he uses his hind legs much more correctly and efficiently. He is more attentive and a lot less spooky.

At only four this is still early days for him, but it is apparent how beneficial Connected Groundwork has been in teaching him how to release and balance himself.

9 Shoulder Press

PURPOSE

Shoulder Press encourages the horse to let go of tightness in his shoulders and the base of his neck and rib cage, and supports him as he bends. It helps the horse overcome habitual bracing patterns that lead to sidedness and crookedness. The horse needs to be able to easily yield his *inside* shoulder by shifting weight to the *outside*, allowing for bend through his body. This bend creates a slight arc from nose to tail, which frees the inside hind leg to come further under the horse ("coming through"). *Shoulder Press* also helps the horse balance and shift weight more efficiently during transitions.

PROCEDURE

→ Begin by standing on the horse's left side facing his withers. Hold the line in your left hand, "snugged up" to the halter, or hook your index and middle fingers in front of the "T"-junction of the halter as shown on p. 64.

→ Make a "soft" (not clenched) fist with your right hand and place it in the fleshy muscle about two or three fist lengths (depending on the size of the horse) back from the point of shoulder. Maintain a straight line from your elbow to your fist, with no "break" in your wrist (figs. 4.24 A & B).

→ Place your feet slightly apart with the right one in front of the left (and closer to the horse) as you begin pressing on the left shoulder with your fist using "2" to "3" degrees of pressure (fig. 4.25 A). As you press, be sure your back, hips, and knees are in *Neutral Posture* and allow a slight rotation in your body—to the left if pressing with your right hand and vice versa.

→ Maintain the contact for a few seconds, then slowly ease off the pressure. The most important part of this exercise is the *slow release* of pressure, as this is when the horse finds his own *self-carriage*—his

4.24 A & B *Correct:* Place your "soft" fist behind the point of the shoulder with a straight wrist (A). *Incorrect*: A bent wrist is ineffective because it causes bracing in your body (B).

own sense of balance without having to brace. Try this routine: Press while counting, "1-2-3-4," then slowly release, "1-2-3-4-5-6-7-8." Notice when you press again that a change may have already happened in the horse. If the horse remains "heavy" on the left, lighten your contact and slow your counting.

→ **Variation 1** A variation of *Shoulder Press* is to maintain connection with the outside line with the pressing hand. (The "outside line" is simply the opposite side's section of the line when you attach the line to both sides of the halter, as shown on p. 38). Some horses need this additional support when doing *Shoulder Press*. This is a good place to start teaching them that it is safe to accept contact on both sides (fig. 4.25 B).

→ When this exercise is done at the walk it becomes *Walking "S" Two Hands* (p. 109).

OBSERVATIONS

As with earlier exercises, look for signs of relaxation, indicating the horse's nervous system is accepting the information you are giving him. Does the horse lower his head? Does his body feel softer and more pliable under your fist? Does it take very little pressure to cause him to shift his weight away from your fist (on the inside shoulder) to the outside leg? These are all signs of the horse releasing.

4.25 A & B My left hand is on the halter and my right hand is in *Shoulder Press* with a light, soft hold on the line. My feet are slightly apart and my body is rotated slightly left. This gelding accepts my contact and responds by shifting his weight to the outside leg, releasing the base of his neck, and beginning to bend his body in an arc (A). I demonstrate *Shoulder Press Variation 1* in B, keeping contact on the outside line as I press.

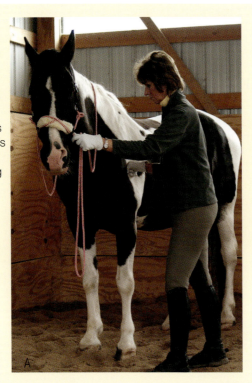
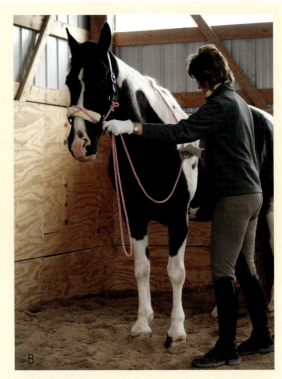

When the horse braces he leans into your hand and you will not feel a "give" under your fist. The horse may also raise his head, back up, or move away from your touch.

Does the horse readily shift his weight from his left leg to his right leg and back to his left leg in response to *Shoulder Press*? The press and slow release "renews" the possibility for shifting weight from side to side and down to up more readily, which loosens his front legs and allows him to then shift his weight backward. In other words, he can move dynamically in all directions.

10   Heart-Girth Press

PURPOSE

The *Heart-Girth Press* gives the horse freedom to release the base of his neck and his rib cage. This allows him to shift weight from side to side and front to back,

helps him bend through his body, and increases the ease and depth of respiration. It helps the horse stretch into contact when ridden. After working with the *Heart-Girth Press,* lateral work and transitions become easier.

PROCEDURE

→ Stand at the horse's left side facing the heart-girth area—the little hollow behind the elbow below the withers. Hold your left hand "snugged up" to the halter or about 12 inches out on the line. Start with your feet slightly apart and your right foot in front of your left. Bend your upper body at the hips (see the *crease release*, p. 32), and keep your back, hips, and knees in *Neutral Posture*.

→ Place your right forearm against the horse's heart girth and allow the weight of your body to press against him. Notice, as you press, the sensation of

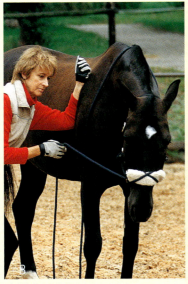

4.26 A & B I stand on the right side of this horse doing a *Heart-Girth Press*, and he accepts my contact (A). As I press, the horse's head lowers as he releases and "softens" through the rib cage (B). His weight shifts to the outside foreleg, indicating he is able to bend through the rib cage and take deep breaths.

4.27 A & B *Correct*: I maintain a light contact on the outside line as I do *Heart-Girth Press* from the right side, which gives this Lusitano gelding additional support (A). As a result, he accepts my contact—note his expression. *Incorrect*: When doing *Heart-Girth Press,* be sure to keep your back "soft" and free of tension, otherwise you'll get a braced and complaining horse, as demonstrated here (B).

your weight sinking into your feet, particularly into your left foot. Slightly rotate your body left. The rotation of your body adds intention to the press of your arm and gives a slight upward sensation to the pressure. Maintain this position for about a minute and then *slowly* release. Repeat two or three times.

→ Move to the right side of the horse and repeat the steps (figs. 4.26 A & B)

OBSERVATIONS

As the horse releases, his body softens under your forearm, he lowers his head, and he may "telescope" his neck. His weight shifts dynamically as he bends through the rib cage.

When a horse braces against you and resists shifting his weight, what you are actually feeling is muscle tightness. The heart-girth area can be a major bracing point in a horse's body, often due to an ill-fitting saddle,

a rider's tight thighs or tense back, or the horse always working on the forehand. When this area is tight, the horse carries tension throughout his body, is crooked and on the forehand, and cannot lift his back or push from behind during movement.

I recently worked with two horses who were very tight through the rib cage and did not use their back effectively. While standing still I offered pressure all the way from the heart-girth area to the end of the rib cage on both sides. On both horses I could feel differences between the two sides—one was "soft" and the other was stiff.

While walking, the "softer" side of each horse was easier to stay with, while the stiffer side seemed to repel my arm. (I kept going back to the "easy" side for a breather!) I did this over three days for short periods of time (10 to 15 minutes) with marvellous results: Both horses improved beyond my expectations, "came through" under saddle, and accepted contact with the rider's hands for the first time ever!

11 Wither Rock

PURPOSE

Wither Rock helps a horse release any tension or tightness in the base of the neck, shoulders, and rib cage. It encourages horses to shift their weight from side to side dynamically. This exercise is particularly helpful for horses that are stiff; lack forward motion; rush; brace their neck; "hop" into transitions; have trouble bending in one direction; or won't stand still for mounting. *Wither Rock* helps horses accept contact from their handler or rider.

PROCEDURE

→ Stand on the horse's left side facing the withers. Your left hand should hold the line out far enough so that you can stand comfortably at the horse's withers. Place your right foot forward and cup your right hand over the withers.

→ Begin a *very slow* rocking motion by rotating slightly to the right, shifting your weight back onto your left foot, and bringing the withers *toward* you (fig. 4.28 A). Pause briefly, and *slowly* take your hand off the withers.

→ Next, again cup your right hand over the withers, rotate slightly left, shift your weight forward onto your right foot, and with the heel of your hand send the withers *away* from you (fig. 4.28 B). Slowly release your contact again. Using your torso rotation, continue shifting from one foot to the other, rocking the horse toward and away from you with your hand. Repeat three to four times on each side.

→ When you feel the horse is "integrating the movement"—assimilating it into his repertoire—repeat the exercise with a lighter and quicker rhythm. Sometimes horses will release the base of the neck, lower their head, and move forward at this point (fig. 4.28 C). If the horse moves forward, *Comb the Line* (p. 51) and walk with him. When you are ready to stop, *Draw the Bow* with *Rotation to Halt* (pp. 49 and 54).

→ After your horse is comfortable with *Wither Rock* standing still, practice the exercise at a walk (figs. 4.29 A & B). There are two walk-rock rhythms that are effective: The first is a slower rhythm in which you send the withers *away for two or three strides* and then bring the withers *back toward you for two or three strides*, and then repeat. The second is a faster rhythm that moves *back and forth in sync with each stride*. What is most important is to feel as if you are moving in time with your horse—not "muscling him around" on the ground.

OBSERVATIONS

When a horse responds to the rhythm of *Wither Rock*, the head and neck immediately start to lower. You can clearly see the horse shift his weight from side to side, and he will show signs of relaxation, such as those mentioned in previous exercises. When a horse *disconnects* during this exercise, he either braces against the movement, backs up, or moves away from your touch. He may also tighten and retract the base of the neck like a turtle retreating into its shell.

When you first begin the exercise, ask yourself the following: Does the horse seem "heavy" under your hand and unable to rock from side to side? Does his head lower? Does he take deep breaths, lick, or chew? Does the exercise get easier and "lighter"? Does his demeanor change after a couple of repetitions? Does he shift his weight to rebalance himself?

If the horse remains unable to shift his weight readily and rock from side to side, lighten your touch, slow down your movement, and ask less. Notice if this allows the horse time to respond to the exercise.

Remember to Remember

Connection originates with your *Neutral Posture* (see p. 20). Use torso *rotation* (p. 54) and *own your elbows* (p. 7) to communicate with your horse during *Wither Rock*—don't pull with your hands. Imagine your motion initiating in your feet as you bring your horse toward you and send him away in rhythm. Engage your core muscles to stabilize and ground your body in order to become a stronger support for your horse.

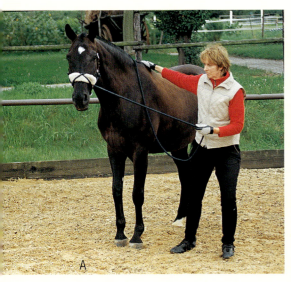

4.28 A–C I cup my right hand over the withers and shift my weight back onto my left foot as I bring the horse *toward* me (A). In response, he takes the weight off his *right* foreleg. I rock my weight back onto my right foot, sending the horse away from me, and he now shifts his weight off his *left* foreleg (B). As you do *Wither Rock*, your horse may loosen up through the rib cage, and as he does, he may rearrange his feet to rebalance himself. When I allow this horse time to process, he squares himself up (C).

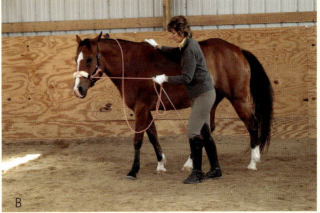

4.29 A & B *Wither Rock* at a walk: I bring the horse toward me for a few strides, keeping my elbow bent (A). Bringing the horse toward you while in motion feels like you're walking toward the center of a circle. When I send the horse away, I feel as if I'm walking back toward the edge of the circle (B).

12 Pectoral/Elbow Delineation

PURPOSE

Pectoral/Elbow Delineation—in conjunction with *Shoulder Press* (p. 77), *The "V"* (p. 70), and *Heart-Girth Press* (p. 78)—helps a horse override bracing patterns that limit his freedom of movement by "softening" or re-elasticizing the pectoral muscles of the thoracic sling so they can actively contract and release. As I mentioned earlier, the *thoracic sling* is a combination of muscles and ligaments that suspend the thorax (chest) of the horse and work as a shock absorber for his front end during movement. When a horse is on the forehand, the pectoral muscles are in constant contraction. *Pectoral/Elbow Delineation* helps release this "holding pattern" and allows the horse to shift his weight toward the haunches so he can find his balance, even with the added weight of a rider.

Release of the pectoral (and shoulder) muscles enables horses to shift their weight up and down, front to back, and side to side more efficiently, improving the quality of movement and elasticity (so they can move like a Slinky™ without kinks). This exercise also eases muscle tightness associated with "girthiness."

PROCEDURE

→ You may find it easiest to have an assistant hold your horse during this exercise. As you begin, be aware that having his elbow cavity touched can be a new and sensitive sensation for your horse. Stand on his left side facing his shoulder. Reach under the chest with your left hand, palm up, near the crease where the left foreleg joins the chest, moving slowly to be sure the horse accepts contact in that area. After a few seconds, gently jiggle your hand on these pectoral muscles. When your horse is comfortable with this, you may proceed with the exercise. Be mindful of your own posture.

→ As you stand facing the horse's left side, hold your right hand in a "handshake" position, with your thumb resting on your index finger. Place your left

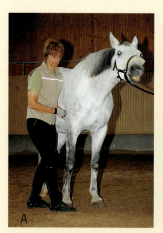

4.30 A & B Here I am doing *Pectoral/Elbow* Delineation from the right side of the horse. This mare was very tight in the elbow area when I began, and she expressed herself quite clearly (A). As the mare began letting go of tension, her head dropped, and she went from tight and tense to relaxed and released in a matter of minutes (B).

hand on the point of the shoulder, or somewhere in the vicinity, as you put your right hand in the elbow cavity. *Slowly* slide your right hand back toward you, tracing (delineating) the elbow cavity with an upward-moving motion. (*Note*: Depending on the horse's height, you may have to squat slightly.) Repeat two to four times.

→ The next movement addresses the pectoral muscles *above* the upper foreleg. Still standing at the horse's left shoulder, place your right hand near the elbow to support the horse. With your left hand now in the "handshake" position, place it in the crease where the left foreleg joins the chest. Gently delineate this cavity with this hand, moving it from back to front and out and upward over the pectoral muscles. You will find a natural groove that your hand can follow. Be attentive to your horse's reaction. Soften and slow your movement if necessary. Repeat two to four times.

→ Next, combine the two movements using a slight rotation of your body to create an alternating rhythm as you trace each area. Delineate from behind the elbow with your right hand, slightly rotating your body left as you draw your hand outward. Rotate right as you move your left hand into the pectoral crease, and then left as you draw your hand outward and over the pectoral muscles. The alternating gliding movements help the horse release tension in this area. Change sides and repeat the exercise (figs. 4.30 A & B).

OBSERVATIONS

When a horse has a chronic bracing pattern, one elbow cavity may seem much tighter, even nonexistent, compared to the other. Notice the difference as you work on one side of the horse's body and then the other. As your horse progresses with this exercise, it becomes easier to slide your hands alternately and continuously. The cavities open up, "soften," and feel roomier to your hand. The horse may begin to shift his weight off the shoulder you are working near and start to "telescope" his neck as you stroke up the pectoral muscles in the front. Sometimes the withers rise, giving the horse a more "uphill" appearance.

Remember to Remember

Some horses may be tightest in the muscles behind and up inside the elbow cavity. If so, you may have to begin the exercise by coming in from the front of the leg first. If the horse seems reactive or uncomfortable, slow your movements and lighten the upward pressure you apply as you move your hand.

13   Spine Roll

PURPOSE

Spine Roll helps relieve stress along the horse's spine and facilitates his ability to lift his back, which enables him to lengthen his topline, strengthen his belly mus-

cles, and carry a rider's weight more efficiently and with greater ease. When a horse's back muscles are hard and reactive (or in some cases, unresponsive) to touch, *Spine Roll* relaxes and "softens" the muscles, allowing elasticity to return. As the back muscles let go of tension, the horse has more side-to-side flexibility, which helps him release his rib cage and shift his weight dynamically. *Spine Roll* is effective with horses that have difficulty standing still, and those that are girthy, drag their hind toes, don't step "through" behind, back up, or pull back when tense. These are all signs of contracted back muscles, often caused by an ill-fitting saddle, overflexion, or overuse of training "gadgets."

4.31 A & B Alternate "rolling" the spine away from and toward you. Here I "pull" the spine toward me (A) and after a count of three, I "push" it away. Remember to repeat on both sides of the horse (B).

PROCEDURE

→ You may need an assistant to hold your horse during this exercise. Stand on your horse's left side facing his back, with your right foot forward. Cup your hands, palms down, about an inch apart over the horse's spine, just behind the withers. Your fingertips will be on the off side. Using "2" to "4" degrees of pressure (lighter if the area seems sensitive—see p. 60), "pull" the horse's spine toward you (fig. 4.31 A). Count to three and slowly release.

→ Next, put your thumbs together nail to nail and place them against the left side of the horse's spine. With your fingers cupped and remaining "soft," use a "2" to "4" pressure and "push" the spine away from you. Count to three and slowly release.

Case Study: REMINGTON

with Connected Riding Instructor Christine Adderson

Before

After

Study Length

Three months

Background

Remington is a 10-year-old Trakehner/Appaloosa cross.

Presenting Issue

Remington came into my care as a troubled, "stuck" horse. His issues included: jerking his head upward, "jamming" at the poll, and compressing the vertebrae down his neck and into the shoulders. He could not bend his body in an arc in either direction as he braced significantly in both shoulders, but especially on the left side. His right hindquarter was also constricted in its swing and range of motion. These physically debilitating movement patterns caused Remington much mental anguish.

Process

My training program consisted of two months of consistent Connected Groundwork. The major focus was in the cheek, jaw, and poll areas, progressing along the cervical vertebrae, and on down into the shoulder. After making marked progress on the ground, Remington has been ridden lightly with a focus on connection and balance, achieving "softness" in the throatlatch area, "telescoping" of his neck, and lifting the base of his neck.

➟ Repeat this movement, rolling the horse's spine *toward* you with your fingers and *away* from you with your thumbs. Shift your weight from one foot to the other as you rock back and forth. Incrementally work all the way down the horse's spine until your fingers cannot grasp the spine any longer. Take the horse for a brief walk and repeat the process on the other side (fig. 4.31 B).

OBSERVATIONS

When a horse is sore or holding tension along the spine, he may react to this exercise by hollowing his back. If this happens, pause and let the horse think about it for a few moments, or go for a walk. Try the exercise again with a lighter touch, or do another exercise such as *The Fan* (p. 85) before coming back to *Spine Roll*.

4.33 A–C I hold my hand and fingers in the shape of an open fan and work from the horse's shoulder blade to the loin area. My hand points toward the withers as I begin the exercise (A), while at the mid-point of the back, my hand and fingers point straight up toward the spine (B). At this point I slow the motions and notice whether the skin seems tighter in this area. You want to use a lighter and softer touch if the skin is tight and the horse seems sensitive. As I approach the back end of the horse, my hand and fingers point toward the loin (C).

I often see horses start licking, chewing, and lowering their head even if they initially had an extremely sensitive reaction. It has been my experience that a horse may show sensitivity two or three times and then he will be at peace with the exercise. I feel this is because he is integrating new information about a different possibility for releasing tension. If his discomfort continues, however, seek the help of your holistic veterinarian, chiropractor, or a bodywork practitioner.

With some horses, you may notice tiny muscle spasms (*fasciculations*) as you "roll" the spine. Maintain pressure until the little tremors cease. When the horse lets go of tension, you will notice the usual signs of relaxation and acceptance. In addition, you may notice the muscles along the horse's spine seem softer and more pliable, and/or the horse's back has been "raised" and his posture is improved. The horse's coat may appear to lie more smoothly and softly along the spine.

Once the horse's back becomes more pliable to the touch, you may find that other Connected Groundwork exercises become easier.

14   The Fan

PURPOSE

The Fan activates movement through the horse's rib

cage by releasing bracing patterns that may be caused by bad riding, poor longeing technique, an ill-fitting saddle, or the use of training "gadgets." Horses are often tight behind the shoulder blade and in the loin area, their muscles atrophied there due to pinching saddles or stiff, braced riders.

This exercise also helps regulate the horse's vital signs during competition and times of stress, such as during travel, confinement, or after an injury. *The Fan* and *Spine Rake* (p. 86) were inspired by a Tellington Method exercise called *Lick of the Cow's Tongue* (see p. 137).

PROCEDURE

➝ Stand at the horse's left side facing his back. With your left hand, connect to the horse either "snugged up" to the halter or about 12 inches out on the line. Slightly cup and spread the fingers of your right hand in the shape of an open fan and place it just below the withers and behind the horse's shoulder blade. Your fingers should point diagonally toward the shoulder blade to begin this exercise (fig. 4.33 A).

➝ Using "2" or "3" degrees of pressure (see p. 60), lift and "send" the horse's skin in an upward direction. This is a very small move, as you are only moving the loose skin under your hand. If the horse's back is tight, the movement is even more subtle as there is even less loose skin available. Pause, count "1-2-3," and release slowly, counting, "1-2-3-4-5-6."

→ Continue this lifting, pausing, and releasing as you work *The Fan* along the horse's spine. When you reach the horse's mid-back area, adjust your hand so your fingers are pointing upward. As you approach the loin area, adjust again so they point toward the loin (figs. 4.33 B & C).

OBSERVATIONS

When a horse is tense in his back, he may not want to be touched at all in these areas. As you begin lifting your hand to "slide" the loose skin, your hand may instead slide right over the skin because the muscles beneath are so tight. If the skin does not loosen within a few minutes, go for a walk and allow your horse to process these new sensations, then repeat *The Fan* exercise with an even lighter touch.

When the horse releases, you may notice more flexibility through the rib cage, and the back and the area behind the shoulder blade may appear "fuller." You may also see signs of acceptance and relaxation, such as licking, chewing, and head lowering. If you see tiny tremors in the muscles, gently support the area with a soft hand until they stop, rather than continuing to slide up the back. These *fasciculations* are a normal part of the process of releasing tension.

15   Spine Rake

PURPOSE

Spine Rake invites horses to release tension stored in tight back muscles and more easily lift their back. *Spine Rake* is beneficial for horses that lack forward movement, suck back in transitions, are "cold-backed," or have a sore back (often from wearing an ill-fitting saddle or blanket). This exercise also promotes circulation in the area you are "raking."

PROCEDURE

→ Stand on the left side facing your horse's back. Connect to his head with your left hand "snugged up" to the halter. Position the fingertips of your right hand just below the spine and behind the withers, and slowly rake your fingers back and forth across the spine, *gently* moving the skin with "2" to "5" degrees of pressure (fig. 4.34 A).

→ Proceed "raking" all the way down to the sacrum—the top of the tail (figs. 4.34 B–D). Repeat the exercise two to four times. Let the horse process or take a short walk at anytime.

→ Change sides and repeat the exercise.

→ Once your horse is comfortable with the exercise at a standstill, practice it at the walk. Many horses really enjoy this (figs. 4.35 A & B).

OBSERVATIONS

When the horse is tense or suffers from back soreness, he may not like the "raking" sensation and may even act like a "girthy" horse during this exercise. He may try to bite, kick, or move away from you. I once had a horse buck when I gently began raking in the area behind where the saddle sits. Should your horse show any signs of sensitivity or discomfort, stop the exercise and let him process. Try another Connected Groundwork exercise and return later to *Spine Rake*, using light, almost invisible movements with only "1" or "2" degrees of pressure.

Slowing down the process and not allowing yourself to become too concerned with the outcome often results in getting the horse to let go of tension more quickly. When the horse releases, you will notice the usual signs of relaxation and acceptance. The lay of the hair on the horse's back may be different and the skin softer and "looser" feeling along the spine. Is the horse's walk freer? Is he standing more squarely?

4.34 A–D Begin *Spine Rake* with your right hand just below the spine and behind the withers (A). "Rake" your hand back and forth across the spine, from the withers to the sacrum (B–D).

4.35 A & B The *Spine Rake* is a very good exercise to do at the walk, as well as the standstill (A). Adjust your hand position on the line so it is about 12 inches out and you can walk comfortably beside the horse's back. My horse Scotia (B—he was 28 at the time this picture was taken) really enjoyed Spine Rake at the walk. The Connected Groundwork exercises helped him maintain his balance after he had a stroke when he was 27. He passed on at age 29.

Cool Down with Spine Rake

After riding and before removing the saddle pad, I use *Spine Rake* under the pad to aid in drying and cooling the back to reduce shock to the muscles when the pad is removed. In this scenario I rake one side of the spine and then the other. After raking the first side, slide your hand up under the pad and notice the temperature of the horse's skin. Then go to the other side and slide your hand under the pad without raking first and notice the difference. This is such a simple exercise, yet it can leave a horse with a released back after a workout, rather than a tight one. I recommend following this with the Tellington Method's *Back Lift* exercise (see p. 137).

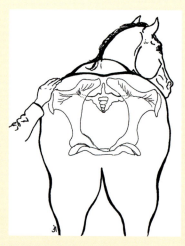

4.36 In *Hip Press*, place your hand over the point of the horse's hip.

4.37 Maintain a connection on the line while you press on the horse's hip as if you are asking him to step over.

4.38 This photo captures the essence of connection! This horse is "soft" and light in my hand, "telescoping" his neck, and maintaining forward energy as we do *Hip Press* at the walk.

16   Hip Press

PURPOSE

Hip Press helps horses create independent movement in their hips, improving lateral movement and maintaining driving energy in the hind legs during turns and transitions. It enables the horse to engage his core belly muscles and shift his weight from front to back (*longitudinally*). This is a good exercise for horses that drag their hind legs in turns and transitions, that fall in or are dull to leg aids, or that have hocks that twist as they walk. *Hip Press* encourages bending through the rib cage and allows the inside hind leg to step through more. Any horse moving freely must be able to move his hips independently or his hind legs will drag and appear unsound and uneven.

PROCEDURE

→ Stand on the left side of the horse holding the line with your left hand from 1 to 2 feet from the horse's head, giving yourself space on the line to reach the horse's body. Cup your right hand over the point of

the horse's hip (fig. 4.36). Press with "2" to "4" degrees of pressure (see p. 60) as if you were asking the horse to step over, count "1-2-3," adding a slight rotation of your torso to the left as you press and count (fig. 4.37).

→ Slowly release while counting, "1-2-3-4-5-6." As you release the press, return your torso rotation to center. Repeat the exercise a few times. Make sure your hips, knees, and lower back are free of tension and that you are in *Neutral Posture*.

→ At any point, change sides and repeat.

→ Try the *Hip Press* at the walk—it encourages the horse to use his inside hind leg with more energy (fig. 4.38). Once the horse has learned to accept some of the previous Connected Groundwork exercises and has an idea of how to maintain connection, he is more likely to keep walking with you positioned near his hip. You need a balance of contact on the line and enough room to reach his hip. Attaching the line on both sides of the halter allows you to do this (see p. 38 for instructions).

4.39 A & B *Sequence 1:* I rotate right and my left hand increases its press on the horse's shoulder (A). I rotate left and my right hand increases its press on the horse's hip (B). Through this "rocking" or "wavelike" motion, the horse is encouraged to shift his weight from side to side and front to back.

OBSERVATIONS

When a horse holds tension in his body, his movement is limited. As you begin *Hip Press* it may at first feel as though your horse is just bracing against you. So after a few repetitions of the exercise, take him for a short walk to let him process and you can better see if he has released any tension and regained quality of movement.

As you press, the horse may lengthen his spine by stretching into contact and lowering his head. He will also readily shift his weight to his other hip.

17 The Wave

PURPOSE

The Wave releases tension and bracing patterns in the horse by inducing movement, reminding the nervous system that sequential, reciprocal, and elastic movement is possible. This exercise enhances the swing of the horse's walk by adding rhythm.

PROCEDURE

→ **Sequence 1** You may need an assistant to hold your horse during this exercise. Start with a combination of *Shoulder Press* (p. 77) and *Hip Press* (p. 88). Stand on the horse's left side facing his belly. Check your posture and place your left hand in *Shoulder Press* and your right hand in *Hip Press*.

→ Slightly rotate right and notice how it automatically increases the connection of your left fist on the horse's body (fig. 4.39 A). Press your fist with "2" to "4" degrees of pressure (see p. 60) as if you are asking the horse to shift his weight onto his right foreleg. Press slowly, counting, "1-2-3," and slowly release, counting, "1-2-3-4-5-6." Often, the lighter you press and the slower you release, the more quickly the horse will "release" right back.

→ Now rotate to the left while pressing on the hip with the same amount of pressure, as if you are asking the horse to shift his weight onto his right hind leg (fig. 4.39 B). Slowly release. Repeat this sequence two or three times. Lighten your touch, quicken

 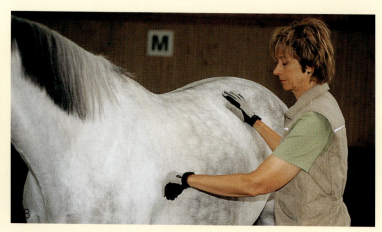

4.40 A & B *Sequence 2:* With my body rotated to the right, there is increased pressure in my left hand in the horse's heart-girth area (A). With my body rotated left, my right hand placed in the loin area has increased its press (B).

your movement, and notice the rhythmic "wavelike" motion between your hands. As you continue the sequence, the movement will become more fluid.

→ **Sequence 2** Now combine *Heart-Girth Press* (p. 78) and *The Fan* (p. 85). Stand on the left side of the horse. Place your left fist in the heart-girth area in the middle of the horse's body and your right hand on the loin in front of the point of the hip. Repeat two to three times as you did in Sequence 1: rotating, pressing, counting, and releasing (figs. 4.40 A & B). Lighten your touch, quicken your movement, and "volley" the horse between your hands. Notice any changes in the horse's ability to move, as well as other responses he may have to the exercise.

→ **Sequence 3** Alternate between Sequences 1 and 2 and notice which combinations your horse responds to most comfortably.

→ Once a horse has successfully integrated this exercise into his repertoire at the standstill, he usually enjoys doing it at the walk. You may need someone to lead your horse forward.

OBSERVATIONS

When a horse is tense, he may be unresponsive—not yielding under your hands as you begin the exercise. If his response is dull in this way, or if he stiffens and/or raises his head, slow down the exercise, lighten the pressure, and give the horse more time to process what you are asking. When the horse "lets go" and accepts your touch and pressure, you will immediately notice the signs of relaxation as you repeat the sequence. When the horse is light and pliable, you should feel like you are "volleying" his body back and forth between your hands. The motion feels springy, elastic, and reciprocal.

What do you observe in your horse when you stop the exercise? Does his head lower? Does he show other signs of release, such as licking, chewing, and yawning? You may notice the biggest difference when you take him for a short walk and suddenly feel that his movement is lighter and more rhythmical. And the walk *visibly* improves—the stride gets longer and there is more "swing."

4.41 The *Tail Rock:* My right hand is cupped over the dock of the horse's tail as I prepare to slowly rock the hindquarters with a gentle rhythm.

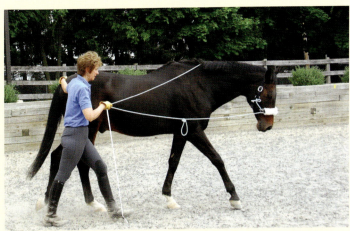

4.42 The horse is tuned in and clearly enjoying our connection while I do *Tail Rock* at the walk. This exercise not only helps horses let go of tension, it encourages them to swing their hindquarters with greater freedom.

Remember to Remember

In all Connected Groundwork exercises, it is very important to release twice as slowly as you take to initially connect. For example, if you apply pressure in an area for three seconds, take six seconds to remove it.

18   Tail Rock

PURPOSE

Tail Rock frees the horse's movement through the spine and hindquarters, and increases the horse's ability to shift his weight back onto the haunches and from side to side. Because the tail is an external extension of the spine, this exercise confers suppleness and greater movement throughout the spine all the way to the poll. *Tail Rock* and the next exercise, *Combing the Tail* (p. 93), are beneficial for horses that are sensitive at the poll and tight in the lumbosacral and tail areas.

PROCEDURE

→ You may need an assistant to hold your horse during this exercise. Before you begin, make sure your horse is comfortable with you approaching and handling his hindquarters and tail. Stand on the left side of the horse close to the tail, place your left hand on his loin for support and cup your right hand over the dock of the tail. Slowly rock the hindquarters back and forth in a gentle rhythm by slightly rotating your body left and right (fig. 4.41). Be aware of how you are using your body, and keep consciously releasing your own joints—shoulders, hips, elbows, wrists, knees, and ankles.

→ When your horse accepts this exercise at the standstill, try it at the walk (fig. 4.42). An assistant can lead your horse forward, or if your horse is *connected,* he may willingly walk forward as you keep light contact on the line with one hand and cup the dock of his tail with the other.

Case Study: PRECIOUS

with Connected Riding Instructor Trisha Wren

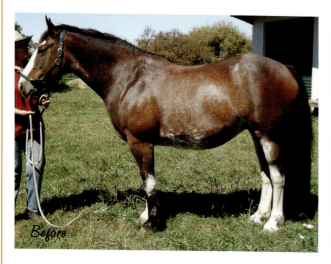

Before

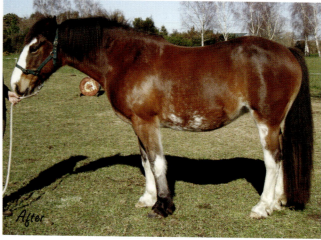

After

Study Length

Four months

Background

Beth Godwin's Clydesdale-cross mare, Precious, is an 11-year-old ex-broodmare with a little experience on the trail.

Presenting Issues

Precious turned out to be very reactive, with a hard mouth and no "brakes." She was also a "head-tosser." When I met them Beth had only ridden Precious 20 to 30 times. The horse was on the forehand and extremely unbalanced. She stumbled regularly, even at the walk, and was inattentive and distracted by her head-flicking habit. She got very upset if she was circled (or longed) and even with the help of an experienced instructor, Beth was unable to get her to circle calmly. The slightest pressure or stress brought out unmanageable head tossing. Beth tried many different therapists and therapies without much success, and she was beginning to think she would never achieve a pleasurable ride with this horse.

Process

When we met, Beth hadn't ridden for two months, and I recommended that we do some groundwork and build back up to riding. Over the next four months I did 10 sessions with Beth and Precious—mostly Connected Groundwork, and only progressing to riding in the fourth month. In between lessons, Beth practiced Connected Groundwork with Precious two to three times per week.

Our first lessons introduced both horse and rider to a new level of body awareness via a series of exercises aimed to release tension and bracing patterns. It quickly became apparent how stiff and one-sided Precious was; even in the paddock she would stand curved like a banana—never straight. She was extremely "stuck" on her right side, and initially objected to us working there at all. She carried her head high and her back and tummy low, and in movement her hindquarters didn't seem to belong to her.

We did a variety of exercises to release her neck: *Cheek Press* (p. 58); *Cheek Delineation* (p. 62); *Caterpillar* (p. 64); and *Shoulder Delineation* (p. 67). We worked to free her spine and lift her back with: *Wither Rock* (p. 80); *Shoulder Press* (p. 77); *Heart-Girth Press* (p. 78); and Tellington Method *Back Lifts* (see p. 137). We combined all these with a few leading exercises, which encouraged Precious to rebalance and engage from behind. Within about three sessions she had started to loosen up.

Beth says, "It was really great to do something with Precious that didn't cause her distress—it became the turning point in our relationship. I started to notice a real difference in her demeanor while she was being worked; she was becoming less reactive and more responsive. This type of groundwork very much worked *with* her, and gave her nothing to fight against. After three months of groundwork I felt very empowered; our relationship had improved hugely, my horse's shape had changed for the better, and she was starting to be more balanced."

After three months of Connected Groundwork, we decided Precious was ready to be ridden again. I started by checking Beth's position in the saddle, and while the adjustments made weren't huge, the different balance and feel made a big impact on Beth, as she explains: "I feel so much more secure, and I am not getting off sore from head to foot!"

I then coached her on how to maintain her position and use it to communicate more clearly with Precious. Precious went from being strung out, inattentive, and stumbling, to engaged, soft, and balanced. "I couldn't believe she was the same horse," says Beth. "She was listening to me, and was responsive but not reactive. I now feel like I have the connection with my horse I always dreamed of, and this is just the beginning!"

OBSERVATIONS

When your horse is tense throughout his body, initially you may not feel a response to the *Tail Rock*. He may even clamp his tail as you first place your hand on his dock. Should this occur, go on to a different Connected Groundwork exercise (TTouch circles and lifts on the tail can help, too—see p. 137), and then return to *Tail Rock* and try again.

In other horses, the tail may be quite flaccid and feel disconnected from the body. This exercise and *Combing the Tail* (see below) can help these horses regain awareness of their tail. When the horse begins reciprocating in *Tail Rock*, his entire body may gently oscillate from side to side as he allows the movement to ripple through his body.

19   Combing the Tail

PURPOSE

Combing the Tail reminds the horse to "soften" in the tail area and relax the tail. A relaxed tail that swings gently with the motion of the horse signifies that the horse's movement is flowing freely through his spine. The rhythm of the combing movement in this exercise adds *oscillation* to the horse's body and aids in releasing tension in the topline and hindquarters. It also helps the horse engage his core (belly) muscles and become more aware of his hind legs. When the tail is not swinging freely—for example, when it is "switching" or otherwise in constant motion—the horse carries tension in his topline.

PROCEDURE

→ You may need an assistant to hold your horse during this exercise. Before you begin, observe how your horse is standing because it might change after the exercise. It may also indicate another exercise you should do first—for example, if he is clamping his tail, I suggest starting with the Tellington Method's *Tail TTouches* (see p. 137) because horses often have trust issues in this area. It may also be helpful

4.44 Stand on the horse's left side, with your left shoulder in line with his left hip, and gently bring the tail toward you. Comb the tail from the middle of the dock to the lower tip, alternating hands.

4.45 If you are comfortable with the horse and are confident he will not kick, you may also stand directly behind him to *Comb the Tail*.

ful to do the *Tail Rock* (p. 91) before *Combing the Tail* to help the horse relax.

→ Stand at your horse's left side, with your left shoulder next to his left hip (facing backward). Reach up to the middle of the dock with your right hand as you rotate your body left. Then slide your right hand down and outward on the tail, changing your rotation to the right as you reach up to the middle of the dock with your left hand (fig. 4.44). Continue *Combing the Tail* by rotating and changing the position of your hands. Remember to keep your knees "unlocked" and remain "soft" in your hip joints. *Note:* When working on a horse you know well and know to be comfortable with you behind him, you can stand behind the horse to *Comb the Tail* (fig. 4.45).

→ Once the horse is comfortable with *Combing the Tail* at a standstill, have an assistant lead the horse in connection while you walk just behind his hip. Observe the quality of his walk: Is he reaching under himself from behind or just shuffling along, perhaps dragging his toes? Are his head and neck level with the withers, or is he holding his head high with tension in the poll, neck, and shoulders? Begin *Combing the Tail* in rhythm with the horse's stride (figs. 4.46 A & B). Are there any changes you can see in the walk as you "comb"?

→ Experiment with *Combing the Tail* while you walk to the offside of the horse and then return to the near side—often, your assistant will feel more energy, rhythm, and impulsion coming from the horse's hind legs into her hands. As always, the person handling the horse will only feel the oscillating rhythm when she is in *Neutral Posture* and is not holding tension in her spine.

OBSERVATIONS

Watch for signs of acceptance and relaxation in the horse after your complete the exercise. Walk the horse in a small counter circle (if you are leading from the left side, walk a circle to the right) and come back to a halt.

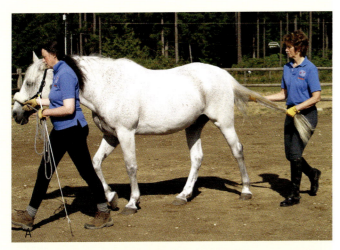

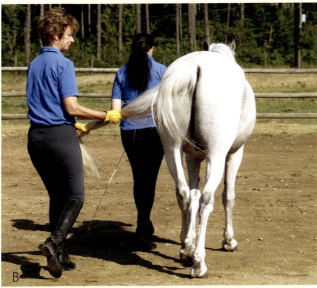

4.46 A & B *Combing the Tail* at the walk is an exercise horses really seem to enjoy. You can *Comb the Tail* in rhythm with the horse's strides while walking slightly to the off side of the horse and then returning to the near side, and vice versa.

Notice if he stands differently. Is he standing squarely? Does he appear more balanced?

Often, the quality of the footfalls of the hind feet noticeably become more accentuated, especially that of the inside hind foot. You may notice more freedom in the walk after you have done this exercise.

20 Sacral Rock

PURPOSE

Sacral Rock loosens tightness in the lumbosacral (LS) area, the part of equine anatomy housing the most important joint for creating and transferring "pushing power" from behind. The LS joint allows for the "swing" of the walk and engagement of the hind end; aids in gait transitions and straightness; helps the inside hind leg power forward; gets the horse off the forehand; and improves quality of stride. It also enables the horse to rock his weight back onto his haunches as he flexes. (To locate the lumbosacral joint, palpate the spine until you find a soft, springy area near the point of the croup.) *Sacral Rock* is a reminder to the horse that he can move freely in the hind end—his primary engine and source of impulsion.

PROCEDURE

→ You may need an assistant to hold the horse during this exercise. Before you begin, be sure the horse is comfortable with contact on his loin, hindquarters, and tail area. Stand on the horse's left side facing the hip. Place your left hand, palm down, on the loin with your fingers facing upward toward the spine. Cup your right hand around the dock of the tail (fig. 4.47 A). Slightly rotate to the right, bringing your right hand and the tail toward you while your left hand presses the loin away (this is a minute movement that comes from your rotation rather than a gross movement from the hand). Hold the position counting, "1-2-3," and slowly release, counting, "1-2-3-4-5-6." Repeat three times and notice any differences in your horse's posture or attitude (fig. 4.47 B).

→ With your right hand remaining cupped over the dock of the tail, move your left hand to the off side of the spine, sliding it over the loin. This time, the fingers of your left hand bring the loin toward you, and the base of your right thumb sends the tail dock away (fig. 4.47 C). Repeat three times and notice changes in your horse's posture and attitude. *Note:* If you are working with a very large or tall horse,

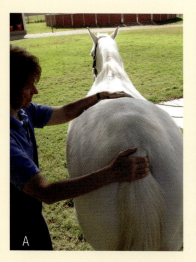
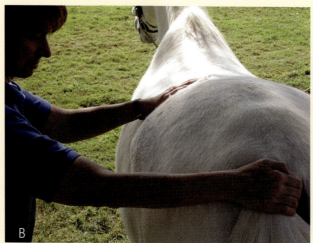

4.47 A–C Begin with your left hand palm down on the loin and your right hand cupped around the horse's dock (A). Bring the tail toward you as you send the loin away in a smooth, synchronized motion (B), then send the tail away while bringing the loin toward you (C). Alternately rock the tail and loin by rhythmically rotating your body left and right. Most horses enjoy this exercise. Be sure to work your horse from both sides.

stand on a mounting block if needed to reach the far side of the loin.

→ Next, "rock" the horse by rotating your body right and left. This sends the spine away as you bring the tail toward you. As you bring the spine back toward you, the tail is sent away. During this step, as with all Connected Groundwork exercises, it is important to "check in with your body" to keep your back "soft," hips released, and knees "unlocked."

OBSERVATIONS

When a horse holds tension in the lumbosacral area, you may feel little or no movement between your hands as you begin this exercise. If this is the case, stop and let your horse process the new information his nervous system has absorbed. Come back to the exercise later and you may find a change the area has become "looser" and more flexible. If the horse reacts to the placement of your hands, try a simpler exercise such as *Tail Rock* (p. 91), *Hip Press* (p. 88), or *The Wave* (p. 89).

When your horse holds more tension on one side than the other, you may notice that the "bring-and-send" movements feel uneven. With practice, you may feel freer and more even movement between your hands.

Remember to Remember

When a horse appears to dislike an exercise or has an intense reaction to it, you will often find tightness or discomfort in the area you're working on. Focus on another area of the body for a while and you may find you can return to *Sacral Rock* with the horse more accepting of the exercise.

21 Groin Delineation

Note: This exercise requires the handler to be sensitive to the horse's possible response to her touch. Use the same precautions as you would when cleaning a sheath or udder.

PURPOSE

Groin Delineation frees the horse's hip joint for greater extension and flexion. It brings evenness to the body's two sides by softening and releasing the hip flexor muscles that connect at the inner hip joint. When these muscles soften, they free the hind leg to lengthen its stride, increasing swing and the ability to push. It also facilitates the horse's ability to step sideways to the midline of the body with a hind foot.

This exercise has proven effective for horses that favor one lead, have more difficulty in lateral work on one side, do not use their hocks efficiently, and drag their hind feet. *Groin Delineation,* in combination with *Hip Press* (p. 88) and *Sacral Rock* (p. 95), is particularly effective for a horse that "corkscrews" (twists his hocks to the outside as his foot lands with each stride).

PROCEDURE

➞ You may need an assistant to hold your horse during this exercise. Stand on the horse's left side facing his left hind leg, but turned slightly toward his tail. You want to be close enough so you can slide your hands up along the inside of the leg. Rest your left hand on the horse's loin area. Gently take hold of the horse's tail with your right hand, and slide your hand 2 to 3 feet down the tail (fig. 4.48 A). Hold the tail throughout the exercise; it will alert you to any discomfort the horse may experience.

➞ Coming in from the front of the horse's hind leg at the low end of the flank just below the stifle, carefully place the flat of your left hand along the inside of the left hind leg and pause to allow the horse to become used to your hand being there. Your right hand remains on the tail (or the back of the left hind leg, if you prefer) to steady the horse and to help you be aware of any sudden movement he might make.

➞ Once the horse is comfortable with your touch, slowly move your left hand up the inner hind leg toward the tail, to the "crease" where the leg meets the body. Using light pressure of "2" to "3" degrees (see p. 60), delineate the crease, moving your hand slowly from back to front (figs. 4.48 B & C). Allow your body to rotate left as you are doing this movement.

➞ Prepare to delineate the crease with your right hand, coming in from the *back* of the horse's leg (fig. 4.48 D). Stand at the horse's hip facing slightly toward the horse's head. Place your left hand on the point of the hip. Coming in from the rear of the horse, carefully place the flat of your right hand along the inside of the horse's hind leg. Pause for a few seconds, then move your hand forward and gently begin stroking from front to back, making sure to rotate your body right while stroking.

➞ As the horse becomes comfortable with this sensation, slowly move your hand forward and up into the crease and begin a light, upward delineation, moving your hand along the crease from the front to the back. During this backward motion, make a gentle sweep outward toward the back of the thigh.

➞ Horses are often soothed by the rhythm of an alternating (left hand from the front, right hand from the back, in rhythm) delineation of the crease where the hind leg meets the body (fig. 4.48 E).

OBSERVATIONS

When a horse displays chronic bracing patterns and does not really "push" from his hind legs, the inner thigh muscles of one hind leg may feel harder and tighter than the other. This may also be the case with a horse that has had a previous injury to his hips or hind legs. Also, geldings may hold more tension in this area because of gelding scars.

Take note of any differences from side to side when you start this exercise. As your horse progresses, expect to notice relaxation in this area. The groin will feel "roomier" and softer to your hands. It is a good idea to also assess the walk before and after this exercise (see p. 43).

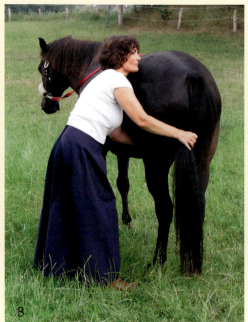

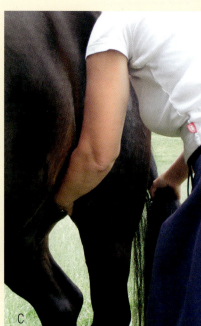

4.48 A–E Begin *Groin Delineation* with your left hand on the horse's loin area and your right hand on his tail (A). Hold the tail as you place the side of your left hand along the inside of the horse's left hind leg (B & C). Once the horse is comfortable, switch hands and reach with your right hand in from the rear of the horse, again stroking the inside of the horse's left hind leg (D). Finally, alternate strokes with your left hand from the front and your right hand from the back (E).

Note: Horses can be very sensitive in this area. The tighter (tenser) they are, the more sensitive they are likely to be. If the horse is extremely sensitive, you may have to start by just resting your hand on the inner thigh. Then simply move the flat of your hand back and forth along the muscles of the inner thigh, adjusting the pressure until the horse is comfortable with your hand being in this area. Gradually work your hand up to the groin crease and continue the exercise. You may want to practice it in small steps. Then you can take the time to coordinate it with being attentive to the horse's response.

Tellington Method *Leg Circles* and *Python Lifts* (see p. 137) are a wonderful sequel to this exercise.

Remember to Remember

When doing Connected Groundwork, allow yourself to slightly rotate your torso so your *whole body* participates, not just your arms. Check in with yourself often to make sure you are standing in *Neutral Posture* with your back and joints released (see p. 20).

PART V
Transitional Exercises for the Horse

Now that you and your horse are proficient at finding and staying in *Neutral Posture*, are letting go of habitual tension patterns (bracing), and are able to accept and reciprocate contact on the line (working in *connection*), you are ready to apply the exercises you learned in Part IV (p. 57) in various combinations. The exercises you are about to learn are the transition steps to more dynamic, creative, and advanced Connected Groundwork and Connected Riding. They require more focus and coordination.

Remember to pay attention to your posture and breathing, and remain aware of continuously releasing any tension in your body—it takes practice as you explore each exercise with your horse. Once you have a grasp of this new series of exercises, you can begin to vary your Connected Groundwork routine. Groundwork, like riding, can be an intuitive dance as well as a schooling activity.

Note: Before doing any of the exercises in this section, review *Assessing the Horse's Walk* (p. 43) and make a habit of noticing how he moves each time you work with him. Your awareness needs to be heightened so you can evaluate the changes that take place during the exercises ahead.

▊ Seven Groundwork-in-Motion Exercises

1 Walking "S" One Hand

PURPOSE

Walking "S" One Hand helps a horse stretch the muscles of his topline. It helps the horse let go of bracing patterns, eases stiffness in his body, and encourages him to readily shift his weight in all directions while walking and changing direction. As the horse releases tension and shifts his weight, both sides of his body become more supple, minimizing his natural tendency to be one-sided. The serpentine-like motion of this exercise also helps you assess your horse's energy level and flexibility on a particular day. *Walking "S" One Hand* loosens the horse's back and rib cage, and warms up his muscles before riding.

PROCEDURE

→ Stand at your horse's head on his left side. *Draw the Bow* (p. 49), "snug up" your right hand to the halter, and slightly rotate your body to the right as you ask for the walk—think *Step to the Offside* (p. 52). This begins the pattern of a shallow "S" as your horse mirrors your movement (figs. 5.1 A & B). Walk four or five steps to the right (without making too much of a curve), then slowly rotate left and take four or five steps to the left (figs. 5.1 C–E). You want the horse to "soften" and lower his head and neck; to move his feet; and to release his inside shoulder.

→ After repeating the "S" pattern two or three times, changing your body's rotation and direction every few strides, walk a straight line (figs. 5.1 F–H). Look for your horse to lower his head and notice if he has more energy and motion coming from his hind legs. If you began with a hyper, anxious horse, you might notice him quieting, whereas a lethargic horse will perk up.

→ Once the horse can do shallow "S" loops with ease, try a deeper "S" curve. As you begin walking right (with you on the horse's left side, and vice versa), start slightly ahead of the horse's head and increase your body's rotation as you turn. After four or five steps, change direction by taking a step sideways to the left, then walk backward a couple of steps while *Combing the Line* (p. 51). As the horse's head and neck come left, step sideways again with your left foot and again move backward to create more room for the horse to change his direction. Maintain a 45-degree angle to the horse to facilitate the horse's change of direction and increase his ability to bend through his rib cage (figs. 5.1 I & J).

→ When the horse's head is pointing toward you, *Draw the Bow* and change direction again, going back to the right by walking forward past the front of the horse's head, rotating your body right and walking on. Make sure your hand at the halter stays soft to allow the horse's head to make the change of direction and

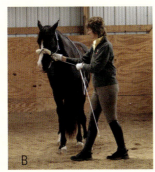
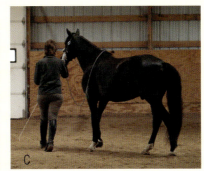

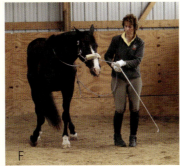

5.1 A–K I *Draw the Bow* in preparation for *Walking "S" One Hand*, then *Step to the Offside* and the horse's head moves with me (A & B). We continue *Walking the "S"* to the right, then change direction through the corner so we are now going to the left (C–E). I *Draw the Bow* in preparation for another change of direction, we walk to the right, and coming out of this curve we move straight for a couple of strides (F–H). Now I step back and *Comb the Line* as the horse turns (I), then raise my right hand (holding the wand) and slide out on the line with my left while tapping the horse with the wand to maintain momentum as he makes a nice bend to the left (J). We pause to allow the horse time to absorb and integrate the sensations of bending and moving we just explored (K).

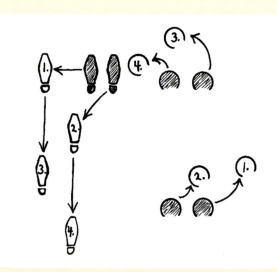

5.2 The footfalls of horse and handler during the deeper "S" turn in *Walking "S" One Hand*. You step sideways, then backward several steps, and the horse follows with his hind and forefeet. Like a dance, the exercise takes a bit of practice to learn the coordinated steps, but once you experience its rhythm and movement in concert with your horse, you will both enjoy the results!

5.3 When the horse tilts or tosses his head, as this horse is, it is likely that his muscles are tense, his vertebrae are out of alignment, or he has a dental issue. Slow the movement down, allow the horse more time to process, or change the exercise. Call an equine chiropractor, equine dentist, or your veterinarian if you suspect issues stemming from teeth or spinal alignment.

stay with you. This particular exercise takes a bit of practice; at first, you may end up walking right with the horse looking left (that is, he is not bending in the direction in which he is going).

→ Go for a walk or allow a break so the horse can process the exercise (fig. 5.1 K)

OBSERVATIONS

When the horse is stiff or "stuck" anywhere on his body, he may toss or tilt his head, wring his tail, or stop when changing directions (fig. 5.3). He may back up as you ask him to move forward on a curve, or he may not want to move at all while you are at his head (fig. 5.4). If the horse shows signs of anger, such as pinning his ears or trying to bite, he may have issues with his teeth, misalignment in his head and neck, or some other source of discomfort. When this is the case, or if the horse plants his feet at any point, let him process and go back to some of the early exercises in Part IV (p. 57). Return to *Walking "S" One Hand* another time.

Your horse may move freely in one direction but be very "heavy" or tight in the other. To help the horse even out on both sides, continue with shallow "S" loops, but do fewer to the heavy or tight side until the transitions become easier for him. Another option is to walk a circle on his "easy" side; as you're walking that circle, take one step off it (toward the "hard" side), then come right back and continue the circle. Next take two steps off, and return to the circle, then three, and so on, gradually increasing the number of steps in the difficult direction by increments.

If your horse barges or rushes through the "S" curves with a stiff body, *Step to the Offside* and then step sideways and backward while *Combing the Line*. Walk an entire circle using this method to divert the rushing, get your horse to bend through the rib cage and take a deep breath, and break the cycle of tension.

5.4 When a horse is "stuck" and refuses to move, let him process, review an exercise he is comfortable with, and return to *Walking "S" One Hand* later in the session or on another day.

When the horse is lacking focus and is high-headed, whinnying for his buddies, or otherwise distracted, pick up the tempo (for example, two quick steps to the offside, two quick steps back) to break up the pattern of paranoia. You'll need to be incredibly light and quick with your hands while you *Draw the Bow, Step to the Offside,* and then *Comb the Line.* This rapid-fire movement helps a horse shift his weight sequentially and brings him back into focus.

As the horse's head and neck "soften," your changes of direction will become more fluid. When walking straight after several "S" loops, you may notice the horse lowering his head, licking, and chewing. The swing of the horse's walk will improve as he pushes off more with his hind legs. Halt-to-walk transitions will also become easier and lighter.

Remember to Remember

The horse's change of direction is initiated by your body's *rotation* (see p. 54). Your hands merely maintain connection to the horse on the halter or line—they do not pull or push.

2   Finding the Walking Rhythm

PURPOSE

Finding the Walking Rhythm awakens and maintains the naturally occurring minute oscillations in the horse's movement and synchronizes handler and horse. It establishes *reciprocity* between handler and horse (see p. 8). When you see a horse and handler walking in connection, what you notice is the synchrony as they walk in unison. It appears as though the handler's arm is doing nothing—there is no noticeable side-to-side movement.

PROCEDURE

→ Stand at the horse's left side, *Draw the Bow* (p. 49) and begin walking by *Stepping to the Offside* (p. 52) and walking on.

→ You are seeking the sensation of a left-right rhythmical pulsation in your hand as you walk (fig. 5.5). This minute, invisible oscillation is the rhythm of the two sides of the horse's body moving back and forth from his hind legs, through his spine, to his poll. This feeling of connection can only be felt when you are in *Neutral Posture*, which allows your own oscillating rhythm to come through from your feet to the horse. When the horse retracts and braces his head and neck, this movement is shut down.

→ When the rhythm in your hand (from the horse) is energetic and forward, continue walking until you notice a change.

5.5 Walking in rhythm appears effortless when you and your horse's movements are synchronized. You desire the sensation of a subtle left-right pulsation in your hand as you walk with your horse—his body's oscillation transmitting to and through you.

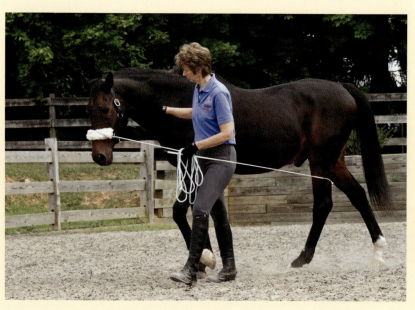

5.6 Walk more deliberately—slower or faster, with purpose—to help your horse find the right rhythm. Here I am walking in rhythm with this horse, and I can feel the oscillating rhythm of his body in my hands, and notice we've raised the same leg, the same amount, at the same time.

→ If the rhythm decreases, your own rhythm needs to become more animated and purposeful for several strides, as if to "turn up the volume" of the horse's side-to-side motion (fig. 5.6). *Do not* push the horse's head from side to side—simply become more deliberate with your own walking rhythm.

→ Conversely, if the horse quickens his rhythm and becomes too strong, "turn down the volume" by slowing down your own strides. You can also go back to *Slide Up/Slide Out* (p. 49), *Combing the Line* (p. 51), or *Elephant's Trunk* (p. 74) to help the horse rebalance and restart his body's oscillation.

OBSERVATIONS

When the horse's poll is free (it moves in all directions— up, down, and side to side, just from the action of the horse's gaits), movement flows through his entire spine without interruption. *Finding the Walking Rhythm* helps to recreate those movements (especially side to side) that have been lost through compression of the spine, which can occur from an ill-fitting saddle, poor rider balance, or overuse of training "gadgets."

When you don't feel the horse's rhythm in your hand, something is "stuck" and braced in his body—or yours. The line may feel "dull" or inactive in your hand, the horse may seem unresponsive, and he may lack focus.

With practice, *Finding the Walking Rhythm* can revive elasticity, oscillation, and reciprocity between you and your horse. The horse's focus will be on you, and his response will be attuned to your slightest movements. These are all signs of *connection*.

3   Topline Stretch: A Combination Exercise

PURPOSE

The following exercise combinations help the horse let go of tension and bracing patterns in the head and neck, stretch his topline, enhance his flexibility, and engage his hind legs. They are particularly beneficial for horses that tend to lose their balance (for example, "fall in"), and they help most horses become more fluid when bending and changing direction. The *Cheek Press* sequence helps the horse stay out on the line and rebalance, release his poll, and maintain an arc during a turn.

PROCEDURE

→ *Note:* Establish all the exercise combinations standing still before walking. Begin on the left side of the horse. *Draw the Bow* (p. 49) by sliding your right hand up to the halter and *Comb the Line* (p. 51). Then *Draw the Bow* again and *Step to the Offside* (p. 52), walking a small circle to the right (figs. 5.7 A–E).

→ Now, *Draw the Bow* and take one *Step to the Offside,* then step back to where you began. Take another step backward while *Sliding Out* (p. 49) on the line about a foot. Then *Slide Up, Draw the Bow, Step to the Offside,* and walk a small circle to the right. What is important here is the rotation of the horse's head to the *right* when you *Step to the Offside,* and the rotation of the horse's head to the *left,* when you step back and *Slide Out.*

→ *Draw the Bow* again and take one *Step to the Offside,* pause, step backward, and as your left hand

slides out on the line, the horse's head and neck should turn toward you (figs. 5.7 F & G).

→ *Draw the Bow, Slide Out* with your right hand, rotate your body to the right, and move your left hand up to the halter so your right hand is free to slide up the horse's neck (from the base—see *Caterpillar,* p. 64) while your body rotates left and your left hand slides back out on the line (figs. 5.7 H & I).

→ Repeat the sequence a few times, and then let the horse process by taking him for a walk. This sequence teaches the horse to stretch his head and neck down to the ground, as he should during a free walk on a long rein. This is a significant part of the horse's development as he learns to "come through" and develop self-carriage.

→ *Draw the Bow, Slide Out,* and as you change from your *right hand* to your *left hand* at the halter, make a "soft" fist with your (now) free right hand and press it to the horse's cheek (see *Cheek Press,* p. 58). As you press, rotate your body left and count to three. Slowly release, grasp the line with your right hand and *Slide Out,* rotate your body right, and *Comb the Line* once or twice.

→ Repeat this sequence. *Cheek Press* helps a horse bend through turns and release at the poll (fig. 5.7 J).

→ Play with alternating the combinations while *Combing the Line* a few times in between each exercise, and notice how the horse responds (fig. 5.8). Use your body's rotation to maintain connection and control the rhythm in the horse's body. Work from both the left and right sides.

OBSERVATIONS

When practicing this exercise, horses often slow down or stop during a change of direction to the inside. When this happens, change direction *again* to reengage the hind legs, and tap the horse with the wand along his belly to maintain the walking rhythm (see p. 111).

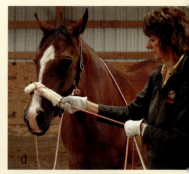

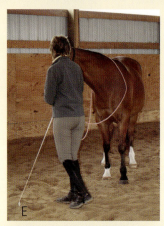
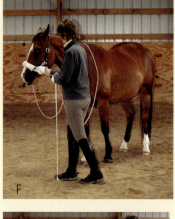

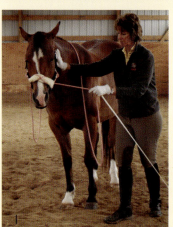

5.7 A–J | *Draw the Bow* by sliding my right hand up to the halter while rotating to the right (A). I slide my right hand out on the line as my left hand lets go of the line to *Comb the Line* and I rotate my body to the left (B & C). I *Draw the Bow* again and *Step to the Offside* to begin walking a small circle to the right (D & E). Upon completing the circle, I take one *Step to the Offside, Draw the Bow* again, and take one step back (F & G). When my left hand slides out and I begin *Combing the Line* again, the horse's head and neck turn toward me. My left hand returns to the halter, and my right hand is free to slide up the horse's neck, from the base (H). As my right hand gets higher on the horse's neck, by body rotates left and my left hand *Slides Out* on the line (I). I repeat the sequence but instead of sliding up the horse's neck, I do *Cheek Press* with my right hand (in J, shown at the walk). This helps the horse release in the poll during a change of direction.

5.8 What *Topline Stretch* can accomplish: At the beginning of a Connected Groundwork session, this mare was so tense, anxious, and unfocused she would not cross a narrow brick walkway. Less than 30 minutes later, after doing Standing Still Exercises (see p. 58) and *Topline Stretch,* this was the result. The mare "telescopes" her neck, stretches into contact, and pushes from behind. Notice the lowered head and flared nostrils.

4 Walking "S" Two Hands

PURPOSE

Walking "S" Two Hands teaches the horse to stretch into connection with the outside line by engaging his inside hind leg. The outside rein also provides a supportive boundary that prevents the horse from falling out of balance with his outside shoulder. This additional support allows the horse to shift his weight in a more balanced manner and bend through changes of direction. This exercise is key in helping a horse bend through his body, change direction more smoothly, "come through" from behind, release the muscles of the topline, flex the lumbosacral (LS) joint, and "telescope" the neck. *Walking "S" Two Hands* sets the stage for positive changes under saddle, including fluid changes of direction, improved energy at the walk, and quality transitions.

Are You Leading a "Heavy" Horse?

Sometimes horses feel extremely "heavy" in your hand—they don't readily move forward, or they feel like a lead weight when you ask them to halt. This indicates they are out of balance in their body. *Elephant's Trunk* (p. 74), *Walking "S" One Hand* (p. 102), *Topline Stretch* (p. 107), and *Activating the Hind End* (p. 113) can help a "heavy" horse "lighten up" through transitions, shift weight off his forehand, and thus become more responsive. In addition, a chain lead such as I describe on p. 39 can increase your ability to communicate with this kind of horse.

5.9 This five-year-old Highland pony (at a Connected Riding clinic in Scotland) was initially very "heavy," "bargey," and unfocused. A chain lead over his noseband combined with Connected Groundwork exercises helped him lighten up and rebalance.

PROCEDURE

→‖ For this exercise, the line must be attached to the halter on both sides (see p. 38 for instructions). Stand at your horse's head, on his left side, in *Shoulder Press* position (p. 77). Your left hand holds the line "snugged up" to the halter. With your

▋ Case Study: PEAT THE FEET

with Connected Riding Instructor Mette Tranter

Before

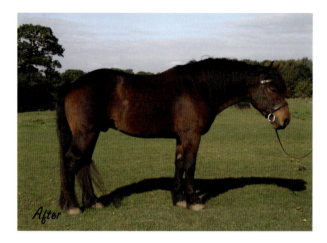

After

Study Length
Three-and-a-half years

Background:
Peat the Feet is a Polish Draught Horse. He's about 16.3 hands tall and weighs around 1,750 lb (800 kg).

Presenting Issue
Peat was given to me because his previous owner could not cope with his behavior when he was out on the trail. He was very unbalanced and would throw all of his considerable weight onto his forehand, charging forward like a bull. If you tried to prevent this he would get very cross and agitated, either shooting sideways or backward at a rapid pace, bouncing on the spot in a very distracted manner, or—as a last resort—rearing. His behavior (combined with his size) could be very unnerving.

Process
Connected Groundwork has taught Peat how to have control of both his body and his mind. He has learned how to "soften" and "give" his head and neck; lift the base of his neck; let go of tension through his heart girth area; and shift weight easily in all directions. This has allowed him to release a lot of anxiety and have a more trusting and comfortable relationship with the world. Since beginning with Connected Groundwork, he has participated in many different activities—from dressage to Pony Club games—and he is a great horse for playing polo as he is fearless. He can even round up cattle!

Peat is now 20 years old. When I first started working with him, many years of moving with poor posture and an unbalanced body were already taking their toll in the form of arthritis in his front legs. However, through Connected Groundwork I have been able to keep reminding Peat how to relax and "soften" his muscles and shift his weight to his hind end. This has enabled him to remain active and continue to be ridden. The fact that he is sound and can still do basic lateral work with ease is a testament to the value of these exercises.

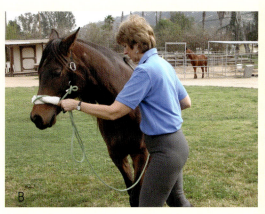

5.11 A & B Begin *Walking "S" Two Hands* in *Shoulder Press* position (A). Rotate your body right as you *Step to the Offside* (B).

5.12 Hold the wand in your right hand, along with the line, and parallel to the horse's body. You can tap the horse's belly with it to maintain the energy in his hind legs as he *Walks the "S."*

right hand, take hold of the line where it comes over the neck from the right side of the horse—it should cross over the withers or just in front of them, depending on the horse's conformation and carriage. Make sure the slack is out of the outside line (fig. 5.11 A).

→ Proceed as if you are *Walking an "S" One Hand* with your other hand in *Shoulder Press* position. Rotate your body right as you *Step to the Offside* (p. 52) and walk ahead several strides (fig. 5.11 B). Halt. Repeat until you have established walking in the *Shoulder Press* position.

→ Walk several shallow "S" loops by taking a few strides in each direction. It may help to "rehearse" the necessary change of rotation in your body at a standstill before walking on. Your change in rotation helps the horse change direction and "softens" the brace at the base of his neck and in his front legs. Notice that when you turn right, your primary contact is in your left hand at the halter. When you turn left, the primary contact shifts to your right fist at the shoulder. Each time you turn left it will feel as if you are doing *Shoulder Press* at the walk. Notice how the horse's hind legs respond to the change

of your body's rotation. Be sure your back is "soft," your joints are flexed, and you are in *Neutral Posture*—otherwise it is difficult to keep your right fist in the *Shoulder Press* position.

→ After a few "S" loops, stop and give the horse a chance to process. Take him for a walk to see if he lengthens and stretches into your leading hand and pushes with more energy from his hind legs while walking forward. You can tap his belly with your wand to improve his rhythm and create more forward energy (see *Finding the Walking Rhythm*, p. 105). Hold the wand in your right hand in the *Shoulder Press* position and parallel to the horse's body (fig. 5.12). Repeat the "S" sequence and as you walk, turn your right hand (which is also holding the line coming over from the offside) counterclockwise (as if turning a key) so that the wand taps the side of the belly two or three times as needed to maintain the rhythm in the hind legs. Walk a straight line again and notice if the horse's walk has changed or if he is able to release and "soften" at the base of the neck. If the horse wants to "telescope" his neck, slide out a foot or two on the line and *Comb the Line* (p. 51) to maintain a connection with the horse.

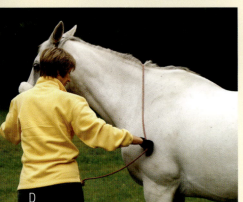

5.13 A–E Here you can see some of the possible ways to connect with the horse in different places on his body, while maintaining contact on the outside line. Play with these as you walk a shallow "S." Options include: *Cheek Press* with the offside line coming over the neck (A); the middle of the neck, a very common bracing place for many horses (B); the *Shoulder Delineation* area—a great place to support horses that tend to fall in on one shoulder (C); the *Shoulder Press* position (D); and a few more inches toward the back of the horse in *Heart-Girth Press* position (E). This and *Shoulder Press* really help horses with bending and shifting their weight dynamically.

→ Repeat this sequence from the horse's right side.

→ **Variation 1** *Walking "S" Two Hands* is not always easy when first introduced because horses often brace when changing direction. To "chunk down" the exercise and give the horse more support, the connection of your second hand (your right hand, when working on his left side) can be made on other parts of the horse's body where you have already established contact in the Standing Still Exercises (see p. 58). Some horses that lack in self-control, or those that can't walk in a straight line or follow a turn, need you to reeducate them one section of their body at a time, allowing them to feel support from one hand at the halter and the other holding the line from the offside, while at the same time you press the cheek, the neck, or the shoulder (figs. 5.13 A–E). It may be that you have pay attention to one area for some time until the horse regains his balance and focus.

OBSERVATIONS

As with all Connected Groundwork exercises, it is imperative that you give the horse time to process what he is learning. It is also important that you observe the quality

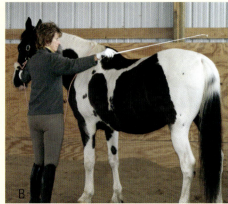

5.14 A–C Holding the wand in your right hand, stroke the horse's back with it (A), then "scoop the croup" to encourage your horse to move forward (B). Bring the wand across the horse's chest to the shoulder on the opposite side and ask for a halt (C).

of the walk before and after the exercise in order to notice changes (see *Assessing the Walk,* p. 43).

Also, consider the size of the horse and the handler, and how that impacts their interaction. For example, when a person is short and the horse tall or large, the handler must adapt her posture to accommodate the difference (using a more exaggerated rotation, for example). It can take a "heavy" horse longer to grasp the exercise and benefit from it (see sidebar, p. 109).

Once the horse understands this exercise, he'll begin reaching into contact by "telescoping" his neck. His walk will improve. Every time you complete an "S," you may feel a surge of energy from his hind legs and a "lightening" and "softening" sensation in your hands, which indicates the horse is truly "coming through." Feeling the energy of your horse's hind legs in your hands is very gratifying!

Remember to Remember

If a horse has difficulty doing this exercise on the ground, he will have difficulty doing smooth transitions under saddle.

5 Activating the Hind End

PURPOSE

Activating the Hind End asks the horse to readily shift his weight from front to back and engage with his hind legs. This requires the horse to let go of any tension in his topline, use his core (belly) muscles, flex his lumbosacral (LS) joint, and step through from behind with more energy and purpose. When the energy generated by the hindquarters is focused, the horse's front end has the ability to lighten, which frees the shoulders and allows the neck to "telescope." *Activating the Hind End* improves the quality of all gaits and transitions under saddle, as well as strengthens the muscles necessary for self-carriage. This exercise involves a series of steps to move the horse off his forehand and onto his hindquarters through a rocking "forward and back" motion. Each time this is done, the horse rebalances, connects, and works from his hindquarters.

PROCEDURE

→ Stand on the left side of the horse, facing his neck. The line should be looped and held in your left hand at the halter. Hold the wand in your right hand and stroke along the horse's back—from mid-back to the dock of his tail—three times. Next, use the wand in a "scooping" motion on the croup to invite the horse to come forward two or three steps (this movement is the Tellington Method's *Dingo*—see p. 137), and then rotate your torso to the right as you ask your horse to halt by bringing the wand in front of him to his opposite shoulder, creating a boundary (figs. 5.14 A–C). Make sure your left hand stays light (*think "up" through the wrist*) as it has to be "free" to move with the horse as he moves. Repeat this sequence three times, then go for a brief walk. If the horse wants to extend his neck, allow him to do so as you let the line slide through your fingers (use the wand to tap if needed to keep the energy coming from his hind legs—see p. 111).

→ Now ask the horse to rein back (back up). This helps the horse rock back on his hindquarters (fig.5.15). Then stroke the croup with an upward motion again, and invite the horse forward. After a few strides, *Rotate to Halt* (p. 54).

→ When the horse understands the pieces of the routine—moving forward, halting, backing up, and moving forward again—proceed to the next part of this exercise. This time when you ask the horse to go forward, add more intention (firmness) and rhythm to the "scoop" so that the horse actually flexes his lumbosacral joint. Do not scoop more than three times or walk forward more than four steps. *Note:* The most important aspect of this exercise is that you remember to be in *Neutral Posture* with hips and knees "soft" and keep your hand at the halter light.

OBSERVATIONS

If the horse has difficulty backing up, return to *Caterpillar* (p. 64), *Shoulder Delineation* (p. 67), *The "V"* (p. 70), *Pectoral/Elbow Delineation* (p. 82), or the first step of this exercise. Review of what you've done will help the horse let go of additional tension in his topline and lift the base of his neck, enabling him to back up more easily.

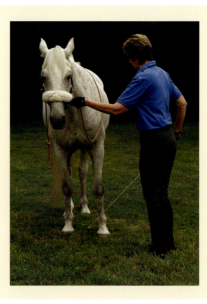

5.15 Backing the horse a few steps helps shifts his weight off the forehand. I use the wand here to tap the leg I want to step backward (see p. 41).

As you practice this exercise, you will notice your horse is ready to move forward with power coming from the hind end at a very light scoop of the wand, halts easily with greater precision, and backs up willingly.

6 Four Corners

PURPOSE

Four Corners is similar to the turn on the haunches (when the horse's forehand moves around his hind end, which stays in place or treads a small arc) and the turn on the forehand (when the horse's hind end moves around his forehand). This exercise is the primary building block for all transitions, lateral work, and more advanced movements under saddle. It helps horses become more aware of their body by asking for straightness and symmetry in their movement via shifting of their weight.

Four Corners helps build the strength of the core muscles and hindquarters while maintaining suppleness through the spine and body. It can help you assess more specifically where the horse holds tension and give insight as to why a horse may have difficulty with a particular movement. It improves the horse's ability to move each leg independently and rebalance more readily. The exer-

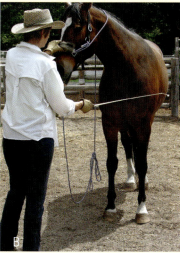

5.16 A & B Start the *Four Corners* exercise facing the horse, slightly to the left of his head, with your left hand on the noseband and your right hand holding the wand (A). Take a step to the left (as you did in *Tracing the Arc,* p. 72) and as the horse's head follows you, tap him on the shoulder with the wand (B).

cise puts a slight bend in the horse's body, which aids in overriding bracing patterns that prevent him from being able to halt easily and release at the base of his neck.

PROCEDURE

→ Stand facing the horse, in front of him and just to the left of his head with the line attached to both sides of the halter (see p. 38 for instructions). Place your left hand on the noseband of the halter, just to the right of its midline. Use your thumb, index, and middle fingers on the noseband to gently support the horse's head. Remember to *think "up" with your wrist.* Hold the wand in your right hand in line with the point of the shoulder, close to the horse's side (fig. 5.16 A).

→ Take a step to your left as if you are doing *Tracing the Arc* (p. 72). As soon as the horse's head starts to follow (moving to his right), tap his left shoulder with the wand in the area where you do *Shoulder Press* (p. 77). Your left hand, thinking "up," passively supports the horse's head and neck as they bend right, and prevents (if necessary) the horse from taking a step forward toward you (fig. 5.16 B).

→ When first teaching the horse this exercise, be content with one step in response to the wand tap—the horse's left front foot should cross in front of the right foot, or even just move a bit (figs. 5.17 A–C). You can ask for one or two more steps if the horse seems ready—his front feet should cross, while the right hind foot pivots or steps in place and the left hind foot steps around it. (This sequence is like doing a turn on the haunches.)

→ After one to three steps, ask for a halt by bringing the wand across the front of the horse's body, touching the opposite shoulder, and stroking his chest. This encourages the horse to shift his weight back onto his haunches. If you are working with a horse that is "heavy" in your hand and difficult to stop, this part of the exercise is very important. In addition, you may have to ask this kind of horse to take a step or two back before beginning the exercise again.

→ Next, stand in *Shoulder Press* position with the offside line in your right hand as you did in *Walking "S" Two Hands* (p. 109). Any movement you request from this position supports the horse in lifting his base (see p. 2) and shifting his weight back so he has independent use of his front legs. Your left hand

5.17 A–C Chico, a 19-year-old Arab-Andalusian cross, had serious problems going forward. *Four Corners* was an integral exercise to changing his attitude and ability to move out in hand and under saddle. In A, his right front leg is crossing over his left. When a horse can cross one leg in front of the other, it means his weight has shifted back toward the hindquarters, he can bend through his body, and his front feet can move independently. In B, we are working in the opposite direction. It is obviously more difficult for Chico to move his left front leg independently—notice the swish of his tail. You may discover that it is easier for your horse to move one front leg than the other. On the more difficult side, I supplement *Four Corners* by walking forward and then moving the horse sideways from a tap of the wand on his shoulder (a "leg yield"). He may find it easier to cross his forelegs with more forward motion involved (C). I then go back to asking the "difficult" front leg to move in *Four Corners*.

should "snug up" to the halter and think "up" while your right hand on the shoulder thinks "down"—both hands begin oscillating alternately and imperceptibly (I call this *Invisible Oscillation*) to prepare the horse to move his weight off the forehand (fig. 5.18 A). Once you feel the horse lighten and shift backward in response to this minute motion, you are on your way to initiating a "soft" and yielding inside shoulder. This means the inside hind leg will better be able to step under the horse's body. *Note:* You can also position your right hand in *Heart-Girth Press* (fig. 5.18 B).

→ Hold the wand parallel along the horse's belly in your right hand, and turn your right hand counterclockwise (as if turning a key). This motion causes the wand to tap the side of the horse's belly. Do this two or three times as needed to initiate the horse's left hind leg crossing in front of the right hind leg—as occurs in a turn on the forehand. One or two more steps can follow as the horse's hind feet cross while the left front foot pivots or steps in place and the right front foot steps around it (fig. 5.18 C). Contin-

ue for another one to three steps before asking the horse to halt by bringing the wand across the chest to the opposite shoulder and thinking "up" with your left wrist (fig. 5.18 D).

→ Next, change hands and lead off with your right hand at the halter with *Step to the Offside* (p. 52). If the horse wants to lower his head and stretch down, slide out on the line and *Comb the Line* (p. 51) as you walk (fig. 5.19).

→ So far, you've helped the horse clarify two transitions. In the first step, the horse shifts his weight back, moving the left front foot in front of the right front foot. In the second step, the horse shifts his weight forward, moving his left hind foot in front of his right hind foot. (*Note: Walking "S" Two Hands* is a great precursor to this exercise as it asks the horse to change bend and keep his feet moving while walking. *Four Corners* then asks the horse to cross his front feet in one direction and his hind feet in the other direction through a change of bend.) Now you can combine the two steps in a walking sequence.

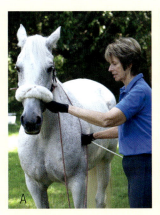 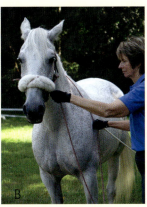  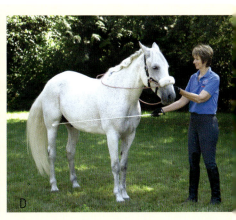

5.18 A–D Position your right hand in *Shoulder Press* and your left at the halter (A). Alternately think "down" with your right and "up" with your left (which shifts the horse's weight off the forehand toward the hindquarters) and then back and forth or in and out with your hands (which initiates movement forward or sideways). You can also position your right hand in the *Heart-Girth Press* position for the same sequence (B). Then, hold the wand parallel to the horse's belly to tap the side of the belly. Do this two or three times to initiate the left hind leg crossing in front of the right—as in a turn on the forehand (C). Touch the horse's opposite shoulder with the wand to halt the horse in balance (D).

5.19 I repeat the exercise from the right side with the horse's right hind crossing over his left.

Maintain the *Invisible Oscillation* between your hands—either up and down, or in and out—and accentuate the oscillation in your front/left hand. Walk the horse two or three strides to the right. Rotate to the left (as you change rotation, move your feet in place for a stride) and increase the oscillation in your right hand while "turning the key" with the wand to ask the horse to step his inside hind leg (the one closest to you) in front of the outside hind leg. Walk two to three strides, then change direction again. You may notice the horse stretching his head and neck forward and down as you walk. You may need to pause, and take your horse for a walk before changing sides and leading him from the right side.

OBSERVATIONS

Assess the differences in the energy of the horse's walk, the length of his stride, and his ability to halt, and notice his signs of integration and acceptance of the exercise. This is a great way to observe differences in the horse's freedom of motion from side to side. As mentioned, sometimes when beginning this exercise the horse is not able to cross his

▌Case Study: HUNTER

with Connected Riding Instructor Trisha Wren

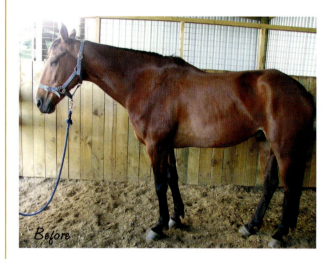

Before

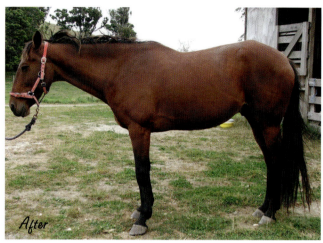

After

Study Length

One-and-a-half years

Background

Hunter is a 12-year-old Standardbred gelding. He raced a couple of times (trotting), and when taken off the track, did some trail riding. He has a fantastic temperament and is very easy going, but deep down he is a bit of a worrier and was quite spooky at first.

Presenting Issue

Hunter had fairly typical Standardbred conformation: He held his head in the air with a bulging *brachiocephalicus* (the muscle on the bottom of the neck where it meets the shoulder); a dip in front of his very prominent withers; hollows behind his withers; a hollow neck; a weak topline and back; a hunter's bump and pointed quarters; and legs that went "all over the place." The general issue was Hunter's extremely high head carriage, hollow back, and inability to use his hindquarters correctly. He was extremely "stuck" and stiff in his neck on the right side; when ridden he felt very unbalanced (he "motor-biked"—leaned—around corners, particu-

larly to the right). When asked to back up, he dragged his hind feet.

Process

In the time I have worked with Hunter he's had (at least) two stretches of about three months off work for a variety of reasons, mainly time- and weather-related. We also had to sort out some dietary issues and some general physical discomfort he was experiencing.

At least 80 percent of the work I have done with Hunter has been Connected Groundwork, and the balance Connected Riding. The groundwork was comprised initially of exercises designed to increase his body awareness and help him to let go of the tension and bracing patterns he had built up. Exercises included lots of *Caterpillars* (p. 64), *Chin Rest* (p. 69) for his high head, *Cheek* and *Shoulder Delineations* (pp. 62 and 67), *Heart-Girth Press* (p. 78), and *Wither Rock* (p. 80) to get him "soft" and bending through his rib cage. The Tellington Method's *Back Lifts* and *Pelvic Tilts* brought his back up and improved his awareness of his back and hindquarters (see p. 137). A year after beginning, I incorporated *Drawing the*

Bow, lots of one-line work, and *Tail TTouches,* which helped connect his back end to his front.

I didn't do any trot work for the first year, as Hunter was still so unbalanced and high-headed in the walk. Once he finally started "letting go" and stretching down, I introduced trot on one line. He is now able to trot in good balance and rhythm. As yet he hasn't managed to translate that to a balanced soft trot with me on his back, but I know that with continued Connected Groundwork he will get there.

Hunter's body has improved dramatically: His back has filled out and strengthened, as has his neck; the lower side of his neck no longer bulges unless he gets really worried; his hindquarters have rounded; and his hind legs are coming under his body more usefully. His temperament has also changed: Where he was a little standoffish before, he now comes when I call and enjoys attention.

front or hind feet. Give him time to process the new information he is learning. If any part of this exercise is difficult for him, slow down and simplify it until the horse is successful. If the horse is "heavy" in your hand (see p. 5), return to *The "V"* (p. 70), *Heart-Girth Press* (p. 78), and the backing sequence in *Activating the Hind End* (p. 113).

7   Connected Longeing: Phase One (Work on One Line)

Many years ago, I was taught that longeing was a way to work off a horse's excess energy, "warm him up," "get rid of the kinks and bucks," and put the horse "into a frame." At that time, the way I learned to get a horse "round" ("on the bit") on a circle was to use side reins. I didn't understand that a horse could learn to stretch his topline and "come through" from behind without the use of such "gadgets" or other forms of restriction. When I began to understand how longeing negatively impacted the horse's body by creating a tremendous amount of compression in his spine and concussion in his joints, I stopped doing it altogether.

Standard ways of longeing often *create* bracing patterns in horses by working them *against* centrifugal force (the force felt by an object—or in this case, animal—that acts outwardly, *away* from the center of the curved path). When a horse is worked on the longe line but has not yet learned to stretch his topline, "telescope" his neck, and engage his hindquarters to rebalance, he inverts (hollows) or retracts his posture, which becomes braced and disconnected. When side reins are used, the horse is forced into a "false frame," the oscillating rhythm of his gait is lost, and the energy from his hind legs cannot "come through." An extremely out-of-balance situation is created, which promotes even more bracing, loss of freedom of movement, and a complete lack of self-carriage.

Many horses can walk, trot, canter, and halt reliably and quietly in both directions on a longe line in accordance to a voice command. However, without *connection*, the handler has no tools to ask the horse to lengthen or shorten his stride; to change the bend in his rib cage; to stretch his topline and "telescope" his neck; or to add more engagement and "push" from the hind legs.

The purpose of *Connected Longeing* is to enable the horse to find self-carriage and help regain his balance when he loses it. You need to create an atmosphere where the horse can find his *own* balance on his *own* feet rather than brace against the line for support. Your goal is to develop the horse's posture so he can move on a circle in balance and with lightness.

Horses that are unbalanced due to immaturity or that have acquired bad posture through incorrect training and handling are often worked on the longe line, in side reins, or with other methods that create or maintain a "frame." In such instances, the compression in their body, the concussion in their joints, the crookedness in their frame, the compensation in their movement, and the resulting evasions—bucking when you ask for a transition, uncontrollable variations in speed, and the like—increase dramatically.

I spent years reschooling horses that were longed in a compressive manner (when the horse pulls on the longe line and you resist, that's "compression"). This motivated me to develop the groundwork exercises you've learned so far. The exercises you have practiced soften different segments of the horse's body so that when he takes and maintains contact, he "telescopes" his neck, engages his core muscles, and activates his hindquarters. This is the posture a horse needs to carry a rider's weight efficiently. The strength for these actions has to be built over time.

Connected Longeing is the culmination of all the preparatory Connected Groundwork exercises presented thus far, and fully integrates them into the horse's movement. It is the "classroom" for basic schooling and conditioning your horse. From straight lines to "S" loops; from curves and circles to transitions and varying length of stride; and from work over poles to basic walk, trot, and canter, *this is the opportunity to create the horse you want to ride*. When you longe a horse in connection, you can assess what your horse needs on a particular day and address those needs from the ground before getting in the saddle.

What I have learned over the years is that in order to have a horse carry himself in an efficient posture at the end of a longe line, I first have to be really specific in teaching him how to rebalance. Allowing a horse to "run around" me with his head up or tilted to the outside only develops ineffective muscling (and poor posture) because he is working out of balance.

The same is true for the handler. You have to practice *Neutral Posture* in your own body as you teach your horse the posture that allows *him* to rebalance. Once you achieve this on the ground, you can begin to repeat the process under saddle. This is the foundation for *any* horse to achieve freedom of motion and realize his potential—as either a recreational or competitive mount.

PURPOSE

Connected Longeing teaches the horse to move in a more balanced posture. It restores and maintains elasticity to the horse's movement. It promotes freedom of movement in the horse's topline and joints, allows the horse to rebalance himself on the line in a circle, and strengthens and conditions his weight-carrying muscles.

It takes a bit of experimentation to learn how to lead this "dance" with your horse on the line. By establishing each of the *Connected Longeing* pieces that follow, you and your horse will progressively "come together" and improve his gaits, balance, focus, and self-carriage.

PROCEDURE

→▮ It is useful to start this work in an enclosed area to give the horse supportive boundaries. A hefty pair of leather gloves (see p. 36) is really useful, especially once you have the horse working at a distance from you. This is because *Combing the Line* is a necessary ingredient in order for the horse to find connection. Initial work can be done with one line attached to the halter on both sides (see p. 38). This way you have the option to use the offside line for support—as if it is an outside rein—as you are teaching the horse to bend and release on a circle, and through changes of bend from the near side to the off side and back again. Once the horse is able to maintain consistency through the cycle of rebalancing on a circle, undo one side of the line so you can increase the distance between you and the horse (see p. 121).

→ Working from the horse's left side, begin with *Walking "S" Two Hands* (p. 109), initiating the walk by *Drawing the Bow* (p. 49) and *Stepping to the Offside* (p. 52). As you change your body's rotation to change direction in the "S," slide your left hand out 2 feet on the line while simultaneously pressing on the horse's cheek with your right hand (figs. 5.21 A & B). Follow this *equal-and-opposing* movement by *Combing the Line* (p. 51) once or twice. Make sure your left arm stays close to your body.

→ Repeat the procedure, but this time, press your right hand against the top of the horse's neck where *Caterpillar* (p. 64) ends, followed again by *Combing the Line* once or twice (fig. 5.21 C).

→ Next, repeat the sequence and press your right hand at the middle of the horse's neck, then the base of the neck, the *Shoulder Press* area (p. 77), and the *Heart-Girth Press* area (p. 78). Each time you press, count "1-2-3," pause, and then release counting "1-2-3-4-5-6." *Comb the Line* any time you feel you're losing connection and/or begin again by *Stepping to the Offside*. Make sure you allow your body to rotate slightly right and left as you press and comb. You are helping the horse "soften" in each of these body "segments" so he can bend and stay on the longeing circle. Think of this procedure as "sculpting" the horse's body into the shape you want (figs. 5.21 D–I).

→ Go for a walk (see p. 59) with the horse 2 feet out on the line and see if he maintains the connection you have just established. It is important to confirm this before moving on to the next step in *Connected Longeing*.

→ When the horse maintains connection with your left hand 2 feet out on the line (at which point you are still close enough to reach the horse's body and press on areas that need to be reminded to lengthen, "soften," bend, and engage), undo one side of the line (the outside of your circle or figure) so you can increase the distance between you and

the horse. At this point the wand replaces the hand you used to "press" various points on the horse's body. You can use the wand to "push" the horse out on the line, engage his focus, or it can point to, stroke, or flick an area that needs to "soften" or bend (see sidebar, p. 126).

→ Begin again with the line looped in your left hand at the halter, and *Step to the Offside* a couple of strides, then rotate to your left and *Slide Out* (p. 49) on the line about 4 feet as you flick the wand to send the horse away from you. As you walk a circle, use the wand in an upward scooping motion as described on p. 113, but this time position the movement parallel to the *Shoulder Press* area to encourage the horse to move sideways and bend away from you on the line.

→ Once the horse stays consistently 4 feet out on the line, use the wand to flick the same areas you pressed earlier in this exercise. This reminds the horse to continue releasing these areas where he tends to hold tension or brace—common in horses that tend to be one-sided. This also helps maintain his rhythm and momentum at the greater distance away from you. To keep the horse from becoming "heavy" on the line (see p. 5) or turning his head to the outside of the circle, walk toward him two or three steps (rotating right), and then step sideways and backward (rotating left), just as you did in *Walking "S" One Hand* (p. 102). Raise your left hand to encourage him to shift his weight backward and turn his head back to the inside (don't pull!) This changes the bend through his body and allows the energy from his hind legs to come up through and stretch his topline (figs. 5.23 A–C).

→ At this point the horse steps under his body with his inside hind leg and engages his core muscles. As this occurs, walk *with* the horse as if you are coming out of an "S" curve and proceeding straight for a few strides. Rotate your body to center and look ahead while moving parallel to your horse. This ensures that the horse "telescopes" his neck and carries himself in

5.21 A–I In *Connected Longeing: Phase One*, I initiate the walk by *Stepping to the Offside* (A). My right hand goes to *Cheek Press* as we walk on in connection (B). I then move my right hand to the top of the horse's neck (C) followed by the mid-neck area (D). Here, the horse "telescopes" his neck nicely. I repeat the cycle and maintain connection by bringing my left hand back up to the halter and *Sliding Out* on the line as I press the horse's shoulder (E & F). This is followed by a press at the heart girth (G), and the withers and back—two other places that can help you "sculpt" your horse's body in motion (H & I). Observe your horse and have fun experimenting!

Remember to Remember

During *Connected Longeing: Phase One*, it is important to keep the following in mind:

Move Your Feet

You must *constantly* move with your horse and remain positioned between the throatlatch and heart-girth area—depending upon the horse's size When you are positioned too far forward or too far back, you and your horse will have trouble maintaining connection.

Add Momentum

In order for you to slide out further on the line and work at a greater distance from your horse—eventually on a circle of 15 meters (50 feet) or so—there must be enough momentum coming from his hind legs. Use the wand to tap the horse's belly as you did in *Walking "S" Two Hands* (p. 109) and *Activating the Hind End (*p. 113).

Build Energy

Every time you have to start the *Phase One* cycle over by *Drawing the Bow* and *Stepping to the Offside*, consider it part of the process of building a residual bank of energy with resiliency and *reciprocity* (see p. 8). The horse improves his ability to change his bend, shift his weight dynamically, and step under his torso with his hind legs. This process activates his core muscles, improving his ability to release into contact, stretch his topline, and "come through" with energy.

Long Stretch, Slow Give (Meet and Melt)

When working your horse from his left side, keep your left arm bent at the elbow and beside your body. The arm can move forward and back with variable degrees of bend, but the elbow should not drift sideways. (*Note:* The same is true in the saddle—when your arms "wing out" away from your torso, the straight line from bit to elbow is disrupted and the "push" from the horse's hind legs is inhibited.) As you rotate your body to the left, stretch back from your left elbow; when you rotate to the right, slowly soften the same arm muscles (see more about *Meet and Melt,* p. 5). As you stretch back with your elbow to *Meet* the horse, simultaneously ask for the horse's inside hind leg to energize with a flick from the wand. The wand does not have to be used every time, and I caution you not to become a "nag" because that might diminish your message. Rotate your body to the right, offering a "slow give" as the horse's head and neck reach into contact. The key to striking the balance of elastic reciprocity with the horse is the correct rotation of your body, "owning your elbows," and *Combing the Line* when necessary to maintain connection.

5.22 A & B *Incorrect:* When your arms "wing out" away from your torso (as I am demonstrating here), your horse will just brace his body and you will pull on him.

5.23 A–F I *Comb the Line* as I rotate to the left with the horse about 4 feet out on the line (A). I rotate back to the right, helping the horse continue to move with a free head and neck (B). Notice how nicely he reciprocates—maintaining connection, straightness, and softness—as he trots a circle to the right (C). When I want to slow down the horse, I hold the line in my left hand and the wand in my right, bring the wand in front of his body, and then move it back toward chest (D). It is very important to slow your horse or ask him to halt without pulling on the line. We switch direction and work to the left, in connection (E). The horse is clearly enjoying his rhythmical dance with me. Note how my feet are always moving, keeping me in line with him (F).

a balanced posture. You want him to stretch his neck forward into the contact that you have so you can "feel" the energy originating in his hind feet coming into your hand. The line seems elastic and alive—a "magical" feeling. This sensation can also be especially apparent in the walking *Caterpillar*, *Walking "S" One* and *Two Hands*, *Activating the Hind End* (p. 113), and *Top Line Stretch* (p. 107).

→ Repeat the cycle—walking toward the horse, stepping sideways and backward, and then walking with him (remember to rotate back to the middle so you are facing straight ahead)—as often as you need to help the horse maintain connection, use his core muscles, and rebalance. Keep your left arm close to your body unless you are *Combing the Line*. It may help to think that your elbow should always be in line with your hip bone on that side.

→ By rotating your body and *Sliding Up* on the line, then varying your hand positions with *Combing the Line*, you can regulate the horse's speed and balance. It is useful to couple this with voice cues and modulation—*"Slooooow,"* and *"Eaaaasy,"* for example. I also use an exercise from the Tellington Method called *Grace of the Cheetah*—a leading position that invites your horse to follow the movement of the wand ahead of his nose (for an explanation of this exercise, see *The Ultimate Horse Behavior and Training Book* by Linda Tellington-Jones—see

p. 137 for information). When you are ready to work on slowing down and halting in connection, *Slide Up* the line toward the horse's head and *Rotate to Halt* (p. 54). Stroke the horse's chest with the wand to help him release the base of his neck so he can rebalance himself in the downward transition (see sidebar on p. 126).

→ʟ As you prepare to slow down or halt the horse, hold the wand in your right hand (when longeing to the right), bring it up in front of the horse so he can see it, and move it toward the horse's chest or opposite shoulder to signal he should slow down ("close the door" to his motion—fig. 5.23 D). By this point, you have done many *Rotations to Halt* in earlier Connected Groundwork exercises, so the horse has learned how to transition from a walk to a halt. *It is of utmost importance that you ask for the halt without pulling on the line.* If you have any difficulty, go back to *Rotation to Halt*, *Topline Stretch*, or *Activating the Hind End*.

→ʟ When you are able to walk your horse in connection on either straight lines or curves, you are ready to practice transitions to trot. Moving your feet, rotation, and *Combing the Line* are the three most critical elements in this step. In all Connected Groundwork, your feet are always moving *toward* the horse, *away* from the horse, or *with* the horse. Your horse's movement—every stride—is initiated by rotation of your body. When a horse has been ridden in a compressive manner (the rider braces in a rigid posture or pushes with her seat bones at the sitting trot, for example) he loses his natural head oscillation. You can use your body's rotation to mimick—and often restore—the horse's natural ability to slightly rotate his head left and right with every stride. So, every transition begins with a slight rotation to the outside (to the right if you are working on the left side of the horse), just as you did in *Stepping to the Offside*. Rotate to the right far enough that the horse shifts his head slightly to the right. Then, step to the side and backward as you change your rotation to the left. This creates more bend

through the horse's rib cage, allowing his inside hind leg to step far under his torso—to the midline of his body. As the horse pushes off on the inside hind leg, his core muscles engage, his back lifts, and his topline stretches.

→ʟ At this moment, *Meet* his connection by giving the line a little "stretch," use your voice as encouragement, and flick the wand toward the horse's shoulder or belly, urging him to move into the trot. As soon as he trots, *Melt* (soften) on the line. Remember to keep up with the horse through the transition—if you want *him* to move, you must keep *your* feet moving (figs. 5.23 E & F).

→ʟ Experiment with using your body's rotation to increase or decrease the circle size, longe your horse in a shallow "S" pattern, or ask him to travel in a straight line.

OBSERVATIONS

In order to encourage the horse to rebalance himself on the line, you must be attentive to his needs—change your body's rotation or *Comb the Line* as often as necessary. As you and your horse become more proficient with *Connected Longeing*, he will readily stretch his topline, bend through his body, and "push" with his hind legs. You will notice the horse "carry himself" for longer periods while you maintain connection. As always, be sure to give the horse time to process during this exercise. Notice if he coughs, shakes his head, or exhales audibly (signs he is releasing tension).

When a horse has become heavily compensated in his movement over a long period of time—either due to poor conformation or improper riding and training—I recommend working on the initial steps of *Connected Longeing*, with the handler positioned no more than 2 feet out on the line so she can touch the horse's body with her hands and closely monitor the horse's posture and tendency to brace. In my experience, horses that at first need close supervision like this change dramatically over the course of this exercise, including becoming sound and/or freer in their movement.

Use of the Wand in Connected Longeing

There are several ways to use the wand in this exercise:

5.24 A Flicking the wand toward the horse's belly helps keep his energy up, maintain his distance from you, and encourage bend through his rib cage.

5.24 B Stroking the chest with the wand encourages the horse to "telescope" the neck or slow down.

5.24 C Stroking the front legs with the wand can slow the horse down, help maintain connection on the line, and keep the hindquarters "pushing" forward.

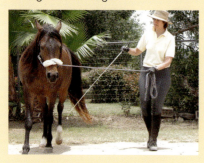

5.24 D Tapping the underside of the belly with the wand reminds the horse to energize his hind legs.

5.24 E An upward scooping motion from the upper leg toward the shoulder creates space and bend, and promotes an energetic, free walk.

5.24 F Stroking the neck with the wand is reassuring, as the soft expression of this mare reveals.

5.24 G Pressing the wand against the horse's shoulder moves him away from you and encourages him to take up the length of the line as you walk him on a circle. This is a very effective aid when you first ask your horse to move out on the line.

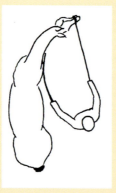

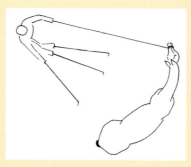

5.24 H There are three places to flick or tap (if you are close enough) the horse to remind him to stay out on the line: behind the ears, his shoulder, and along his rib cage.

Remember: When the horse has a hard time maintaining a connection on the line, repeat *Caterpillar* followed by *Topline Stretch* to encourage the horse to "telescope" into contact. Return to *Walking "S" Two Hands* and ensure that as you change your rotation the horse changes his bend and maintains energy in his hind legs. This is necessary in order for him to stretch into the contact. It takes practice on your part to learn to keep the connection with your body rotation, *Combing the Line,* and using the wand to remind the horse to engage his hind legs and bend. With practice, *Connected Longeing* will become a wonderfully rhythmical "dance" (figs. 5.25 A & B).

5.25 A & B Faisal, a Warmblood cross, works in balance and connection on one line at the walk (A). At the trot, I raise my hand slightly to rebalance Faisal and encourage him to rotate his head toward me. Here he is stretching his topline nicely and "coming through" at the trot (B). This is when Connected Longeing feels like a "dance"!

Remember to Remember

The detail you must be most conscious of while *Connected Longeing* is to keep the arm that is holding the line by your side with the elbow bent and in line with your hip—unless it is extending (opening) toward the horse while following his movement or Combing the Line. The elbow then always works in a forward-and-back movement, and never "opens" to the side. This allows the horse to feel support and consistency through the line. (See more on this in the sidebar on p. 123.)

Case Study: AZENHA DE MARIPA

with Bobbie Jo Lieberman and Nancy Williams

Before

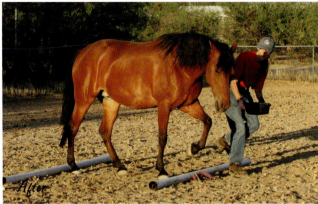

After

Study Length
Two months

Background
Azenha de Maripa is a six-year-old Mangalarga Marchador mare imported from Brazil as a two-year-old by Summerwind Marchadors. After time as a broodmare and trail horse, she came to southern Arizona and is training for endurance riding.

Presenting Issue
Azenha was sweet and friendly, but quite reactive and quick with her front feet—typical of her Spanish heritage. She had several painful encounters with cactus spikes known as "jumping cholla" and became distrustful of humans when they tried to remove the barbs from her muzzle and legs. During groundwork sessions, she was often agitated, grinding her teeth and switching her tail. Under saddle, she would barge ahead with quick strides, holding her tail clamped tightly to her body.

Process
Over a period of several weeks, we combined Connected Groundwork exercises and the Tellington Method to deal with Azenha's issues. In the arena, we worked with *Walking "S" One-* and *Two-Handed* to slow her strides and practiced halting in balance. Azenha has a very quick natural walk, but she soon understood a light signal from the wand on her chest to mean taking shorter steps.

In early groundwork sessions she was reluctant to walk over or between ground poles, appearing almost fearful of them. We did *Cheek Press, Cheek Delineation,* and *Caterpillar*—exercises that encourage head-lowering and release—while she stood between poles. By the end of the first session, she was comfortable with the ground poles and willing to approach them from any direction, stop anywhere during the process, and stand quietly, licking and chewing. We did freework over the poles without a halter or tack of any kind, which she really enjoyed.

We observed that Azenha is very "transparent"—i.e., it is easy to tell when she is concerned about something, and equally apparent when she has accepted it. Her posture, head/neck level, breathing, and licking and chewing all clearly transmit her emotions and opinions.

With Azenha, we quickly learned to engage her without expectations about the day's sessions. She would be sweet and willing one day; wary and aloof the next. When I can "release my expectations," she most often rewards me with a calm, attentive attitude. In our work under saddle, I now make every effort to do this, as well as breathe and stay loose.

Now that you have played with, experimented with, and practiced the groundwork exercises in this book, you have a better understanding of your horse's movement patterns, and you have found ways to help him move more efficiently. You have also discovered that when you use your body in *Neutral Posture*, you are much more supportive to your horse.

I hope you have enjoyed watching your horse release his tension and bracing patterns as he strengthens, learns to balance himself, and discovers how to "power up" from his hindquarters. In just a few months, it is truly astonishing to see a horse's body redevelop and become more flexible and fluid in movement. The best part is watching a horse's self-esteem improve, as does his posture and way of going.

The key points I would like you to "remember to remember" about Connected Groundwork are as follows:

→ Being in "neutral" with your body is essential to effective, clear communication with your horse's body.

→ When something feels like "too much," do less. Return to an exercise or movement that was easier and less complicated.

→ Vary your groundwork routine—keep it alive and interesting for you and your horse. Notice what happens when you change up your level of connection, your rhythm, and the combination of exercises. Put on some background music and have fun with the exercises!

→ Allow the horse time to respond to what you're doing and asking—let him process and take a breath, while you're taking one, too.

→ Work from both sides of the horse's body—it keeps you both flexible and balanced.

→ Remain curious and observant when doing groundwork. Notice that each day you have a "different" horse—apply the exercises that support his body on that day, depending upon what he needs.

In the work you have done so far, have you noticed how the groundwork becomes a "dance" and a reciprocal conversation with the horse? It really does prepare you for a similar exchange under saddle. The same body usage and same principles of engagement and connection apply.

I have spent years, and worked with hundreds of horses, developing these exercises to help riders truly "warm up" and tune up the horse's body in a healthy and more effective way. This helps you maintain the flexibility, elasticity, and freedom of movement that leads to health, longevity, and many more years of riding pleasure. It is with great pleasure and satisfaction that I pass this information along to you.

ACKNOWLEDGMENTS

This book represents years of collaboration with horses, and with people whose support allowed me to bring *Connected Groundwork* to fruition. I am blessed and grateful for the wonderful community of people who share my vision of evolving the connection between horse and human.

For this volume of work, the following people (and their equine partners) have faithfully and devotedly spent many days reading and reworking the exercises with me:

Editor and wordsmith, Bobbie Jo Lieberman (www. bobbiejo.smugmug.com). Bobbie is my "outside rein" of support—she enables my writing projects to flourish and come through to the finish line. I relied on her years of writing and editing experience to capably weave and connect the pieces of this work with me. She restored the fun and creativity to an arduous project.

Readers and collaborators, including Connected Riding® instructors Mette Tranter, Jillian Kreinbring, and Lindsay Cummings; Susan Cook; Feldenkrais instructor (CK) Karen Pelletreau; and Joan and Dan Thompson. Jillian, Mette, and Karen spent countless hours reading and editing many of the exercises with me, and I am indebted to them for their contributions. I would not have been able to complete this project without their help and constant support.

My son Adam Cummings helped immeasurably to bring the book together and organize the images and captions.

Lynne Glazer (www.photo.lynnesite.com), whose photographs utilized in this book were taken in the years 2003 and 2004. As you can see on her Web site, her work has since greatly expanded and evolved.

Trish Rogatzki, Nancy Camp, Christina Dietmann (www.christinadietmann.com), and Klaus urgen Guni, all took many, many photos to capture the moments we needed to illustrate this book. Trish also spent days organizing my photo library on my computer. Final photo retakes were provided by a dear friend and wonderful graphic artist, Melanie Powell (www.shybuckstudios.com).

Equine models include: Q (Celesteele) and Ember (Remember Me) owned by Lynne Glazer; Marrukah Snow owned by Valerie Power; Perle owned by Bobbie Lieberman; Chico owned by Lana Gillis; Joram owned by Bibi Degn, Connected Riding® practitioner; Party owned by Martha Lubow; and Scotia and Belle, my own horses.

Illustrations were provided by Nancy Camp, Connected Riding® instructor, Whole Horse Training (www. wholehorsetraining.com) and cartoons by Sally Spencer, friend, clinic host in Cumbria (United Kingdom), and someone who keeps us laughing until the tears roll down our cheeks!

Thanks to those who contributed the Case Studies: Trisha Wren, Connected Riding® instructor (www. trishawren.com); Chris Adderson, Dance Equus (www. forethehorse.com), Connected Riding® instructor; Jillian Kreinbring, Connected Riding® practitioner; and Bobbie Jo Lieberman, my co-writer.

And for their moral support and unending encouragement, holders of "the vision" Susan Cook and Lana Gillis.

"Peggy Cummings' groundwork approach brings you and your horse into an equal partnership. The exercises emphasize biomechanics, timing, and reciprocation, and facilitate learning by using a non-threatening, supportive environment for both you and your horse. You learn to observe, assess, and guide your horse through your own body movements. With practice, your horse becomes an 'extension of your intention,' making each transition from groundwork to Riding easier because you have gained a greater understanding of what you want from your horse and how to achieve it. It's truly a remarkable approach!"

—Karen Pelletrau, Feldenkrais Practitioner

"I have used several of Peggy's groundwork exercises on my horses. The exercises improve their movement, and I find I have a much clearer connection with their mind. I have attended several of Peggy's clinics, and each time I have enjoyed her knowledgeable, kind, and sensitive approach to teaching and training."

—Karen Cheeke, Dressage Rider

"I've used Peggy's Connected Groundwork with my young horses in training, as well as my competition horses. What I've found is that with just 10 to 15 minutes of work on the ground, I have a horse that is calm, listening to me, and moving from the hind end *before* I mount up. It is truly amazing work!"

—Naomi Preston, TTEAM Practitioner and Champion Endurance Rider

"Peggy's ground exercises do such a wonderful job of outlining the problems a horse has with straightness/stiffness—and then *corrects* those problems. [Her methods] are miraculous and fast!"

—Carolyn Libby, Dressage Rider, and Human and Horse Health Practitioner

"My five-year-old horse appeared to have a 'chronic stifle weakness' issue; after the first day of doing Connected Groundwork, the stifle 'weakness' disappeared and I haven't seen it since (now over four years!) I teach Connected Groundwork as part of my 'basic body maintenance' for my clients and their horses."

—Trudy Johnson, Instructor and Energy Medicine Practitioner

"Because of Connected Groundwork, my horses and I are moving better and are more balanced. The horses are using themselves correctly and are sounder! I am saving money on vet bills and my horses are happier—I am thrilled!"

—Lornie Forbes, Owner, Trainer, Event Rider

"Connected Groundwork is an exceptional tool that we as riders can use to enhance the physical and mental state of the horse. Horses can learn biomechanically correct movement patterns more easily without the undue stress of a rider on their back. This is critical particularly when horses have been injured, are older, or just ridden without mindfulness. Connected Groundwork has enabled me to bring a horse that was lame for 2½ months, with no particular trauma, out of his lameness in just 10 days. We did only groundwork for 45 minutes a day and by day 10, he was completely sound. I am forever grateful. As a physical therapist and Pilates instructor who specializes in orthopedics, I am extremely impressed with Peggy's work. She teaches the idea of 'feel' better than any other practitioner I have ever worked with. I wish I had learned this information 10 years ago."

—Julie Staub, PT, ATC, STOTT PILATES Certified Instructor Trainer

"What excites me about Peggy's work is that both humans and horses change their ability to function more efficiently and correctly. This is achieved in a way that makes each horse and human want to continue the process because [her methods] work with the body's structure, allowing and encouraging natural alignment."

—Hoppy Stearns, E.D.O., Certified Practitioner by the Vluggen Institute for Equine Osteopathy

"The choice of a teacher means the following to me: the difference between education and misguidance; the difference between competence and a perpetuation of ignorance; the difference between a harmonious relationship with one's horse and disharmony because of lack of understanding the horse; the difference between sound, healthy horses and lame, unhappy horses; the difference between happy, well-functioning riders and riders on a downward spiral of habitually degrading movements. My choice of a teacher has an extreme reverence for the horse and a humbleness and open-mindedness in spite of great competence and experience, not only with horses, but in other situations. My choice of a teacher would be a true teacher and mentor—able and willing, with a true desire to guide me along my lifelong path to becoming the best horseperson I can be. My choice of teacher...Peggy Cummings!"

—Chris Adderson, Riding Instructor

"Connected Groundwork gives me a positive way to effectively calm and focus my horse in stressful situations. Whether we go to a show or an unfamiliar place on a windy day, using Connected Groundwork helps my horse physically, mentally, and emotionally."

—Debby Hadden, Riding Instructor and Avid Foxhunter

"Connected Groundwork has helped me become acutely aware of the areas where my horses hold tension and stiffness. The more I practice and perfect the techniques, the greater the benefits to both my horse and myself. I am very happy with the results and I have only just begun!"

—Lori Bridges, Rider

The following common riding and behavior issues can often benefit from the practice of the Connected Groundwork exercises listed below them. I suggest, however, that you experiment with *all* the exercises presented in this book to find what works best for your horse.

Behind the vertical (overbent, overflexed)

Caterpillar (p. 64), Chin Rest (p. 69), Cheek Delineation (p. 62), Cheek Press (p. 58), Elephant's Trunk (p. 74), Slide Up/Slide Out (p. 49), Topline Stretch (p. 107)

Bucking

Caterpillar (p. 64), Shoulder Delineation (p. 67), Shoulder Press (p. 77), Heart-Girth Press (p. 78), Spine Roll (p. 83), Spine Rake (p. 86), The "V" (p. 70), Pectoral-Elbow Delineation (p. 82), Topline Stretch (p. 107), Walking "S" One Hand (p. 102), Four Corners (p. 114)

Cinchy/girthy

Heart-Girth Press (p. 78), Shoulder Press (p. 77), Spine Rake (p. 86), Spine Roll (p. 83), The Fan (p. 85), The Wave (p. 89), The "V" (p. 70), Pectoral-Elbow Delineation (p. 82)

Difficulty changing direction

Caterpillar (p. 64), Tracing the Arc (p. 72), Elephant's Trunk (p. 74), Cheek Press (p. 58), Cheek Delineation (p. 62), The "V" (p. 70), Pectoral-Elbow Delineation (p. 82), The Wave (p. 89), Walking "S" One Hand (p. 102), Topline Stretch (p. 107), Four Corners (p. 114), Walking "S" Two Hands (p. 109)

Difficulty halting

Caterpillar (p. 64), Shoulder Press (p. 77), Shoulder Delineation (p. 67), Slide Up/Slide Out (p. 49), Elephant's Trunk (p. 74), Tracing the Arc (p. 72), The "V" (p. 70), Walking "S" One Hand (p. 102), Four Corners (p. 114), Activating the Hind End (p. 113)

Falling in or out

Wither Rock (p. 80), Shoulder Press (p. 77), Cheek Press (p. 58), Shoulder Delineation (p. 67), The "V" (p. 70), Pectoral-Elbow Delineation (p. 82), Heart-Girth Press (p. 78), The Fan (p. 85), Walking "S" Two Hands (p. 109), Topline Stretch (p. 107)

High head and/or hollow back

Caterpillar (p. 64), Shoulder Delineation (p. 67), The "V" (p. 70), Heart-Girth Press (p. 78), Pectoral-Elbow Delineation (p. 82), Wither Rock (p. 80), Cheek Press (p. 58), Elephant's Trunk (p. 74), The Wave (p. 89), Topline Stretch (p. 107)

Kicking

Spine Rake (p. 86), Spine Roll (p. 83), Hip Press (p. 88), The Fan (p. 85), Sacral Rock (p. 95), Tail Rock (p. 91), Groin Delineation (p. 96), Heart-Girth Press (p. 78), Combing the Tail (p. 93)

Leaning while standing (for farrier, for example)

Wither Rock (p. 80), Shoulder Delineation (p. 67), Caterpillar (p. 64), Elephant's Trunk, Shoulder Press (p. 77), Sacral Rock (p. 95), The "V" (p. 70), Heart-Girth Press (p. 78), Tracing the Arc (p. 72)

Pulling back

Slide Up/Slide Out (p. 49), Combing the Line (p. 51), Shoulder Delineation (p. 67), Chin Rest (p. 69), Caterpillar (p. 64), The "V" (p. 70), Heart-Girth Press (p. 78), Pectoral-Elbow Delineation (p. 82), Walking "S" One Hand (p. 102), Topline Stretch (p. 107)

Rushing/barging

Cheek Press (p. 58), Caterpillar (p. 64), Shoulder Delineation (p. 67), Slide Up/Slide Out (p. 49), Elephant's Trunk (p. 74), Heart-Girth Press (p. 78), The Fan (p. 85), Spine Rake (p. 86), Combing the Line (p. 51)

"Sticky" in transitions

Caterpillar (p. 64), Wither Rock (p. 80), The "V" (p. 70), Heart-Girth Press (p. 78), Hip Press (p. 88), Sacral Rock (p. 95), The Wave (p. 89), Slide Up/Slide Out (p. 49), Topline Stretch (p. 107), Walking "S" Two Hands (p. 109), Activating the Hind End (p. 113)

"Sucking back"

Caterpillar (p. 64), Wither Rock (p. 80), Shoulder Delineation (p. 67), Heart-Girth Press (p. 78), Elephant's Trunk (p. 74), Slide Up/Slide Out (p. 49), Topline Stretch (p. 107)

Trouble standing still

Combing the Line (p. 51), Caterpillar (p. 64), Shoulder Delineation (p. 67), The Wave (p. 89), Elephant's Trunk (p. 74), Heart-Girth Press (p. 78), Tail Rock (p. 91), Combing the Tail (p. 93), Walking "S" One Hand (p. 102), Four Corners (p. 114), Walking "S" Two Hands (p. 109)

Trouble with trailer loading

Heart-Girth Press (p. 78), Wither Rock (p. 80), Shoulder Delineation (p. 67), Caterpillar (p. 64), Hip Press (p. 88), Cheek Press (p. 58), The "V" (p. 70), Walking "S" One Hand (p. 102), Four Corners (p. 114), Topline Stretch (p. 107), Activating the Hind End (p. 113)

RECOMMENDED READING

Connected Riding®: An Introduction by Peggy Cummings with Diana Deterding (Primedia Equine Group, 1999).

Connected Riding and Groundwork—DVD (pferdiatv, Thomas Vogel, 2007).

The Horse's Muscles in Motion by Sara Wyche (Crowood Press, 2002)

Know Your Horse Inside Out by Sarah Fisher (David and Charles Ltd., 2007).

Principles of Conformation Analysis, Volumes 1–3 by Deb Bennett, PhD (Fleet Street Publishing, 1991).

Tug of War: Classical versus "Modern" Dressage by Dr. Gerd Heuschmann (Trafalgar Square Books, 2008).

The Ultimate Horse Behavior and Training Book by Linda Tellington-Jones with Bobbie Jo Lieberman (Trafalgar Square Books, 2006).

RESOURCES

Connected Enterprises, Inc.
PO Box 1627
Poulsbo, WA 983703
800.310.2192
www.connectedriding.com

Feldenkrais Educational Foundation of North American (FEFNA)
3611 SW Hood Ave., Suite 100
Portland, OR 97239
866.333.6248 or 503.221.6612
www.feldenkrais.com

Tellington TTouch Training
PO Box 3793
Santa Fe, NM 87501
866.4.TOUCH
www.ttouch.com

ABOUT PEGGY CUMMINGS

Even as a high school student, Peggy Cummings knew—experientially and intuitively—that something was keeping the school horses she rode and worked with from expressing their innate curiosity, trust, and freedom of motion. Although she often heard the words "lightness and ease" from her instructors and in classical texts, and had the opportunity to ride high-level horses, she saw that many horses were shut down and lifeless, going about their work in a mechanical, stiff way.

Helping her first horse King regain his trust, playfulness, and self-carriage became the foundation of a lifetime of dedication to helping horses and riders achieve freedom from the bracing patterns and tension that so often dampen the joy that attracts us to horses in the first place.

As she began traveling and teaching clinics, Peggy was beginning to chart her own path, teaching her students to ride with more awareness, lightness, and softness in their body. Her mentors, Sally Swift, Linda Tell-ington-Jones, Major Anders Lingren, and others, further helped Peggy shift the riding paradigm from "cramming and jamming" to a new model of horsemanship—one that honors horses out of knowledge and balance rather than fear or force.

Photo by jmsphotoimagery

Today in clinics world-wide and through her Web site and books, Peggy helps countless riders discover their own "aha" moments, helping horses and riders get "unstuck", regain their elasticity, and learn what it's like to move without bracing patterns, compression, and counterbalancing. Thirty years after Peggy learned how to influence her horse King without even sitting on him, Connected Groundwork and Connected Riding became her answers to this universal riding dilemma.

INDEX